Decks & Decking

Decks & Decking

15 step-by-step projects

Quick and easy ideas to enhance your garden

Alan & Gill Bridgewater

NEW HOLLAND

First published in 2003 by New Holland Publishers (UK) Ltd
London · Cape Town · Sydney · Auckland

Garfield House, 86–88 Edgware Road, London W2 2EA, United Kingdom
www.newhollandpublishers.com

80 McKenzie Street, Cape Town 8001, South Africa

Level 1, Unit 4, 14 Aquatic Drive, Frenchs Forest, NSW 2086, Australia

218 Lake Road, Northcote, Auckland, New Zealand

ISBN 1 84330 471 6

1 3 5 7 9 10 8 6 4 2

Editorial Direction: Rosemary Wilkinson
Project Editor: Clare Johnson
Production: Hazel Kirkman

Designed and created for New Holland by AG&G BOOKS
Project design: AG&G Books   Project construction: AG&G Books and John Heming
Planting and props: AG&G Books and Vana Haggerty
Photography: AG&G Books and Ian Parsons   Illustrator: Gill Bridgewater
Editor: Fiona Corbridge   Designer: Glyn Bridgewater

Reproduction by Pica Digital Pte Ltd, Singapore
Printed and bound in Malaysia by Times Offset (M) Sdn. Bhd.

The information in this book is true and complete to the best of our knowledge. All recommendations are
made without guarantee on the part of the authors and the publishers. The authors and publishers
disclaim any liability for damages or injury resulting from the use of this information.

Conversion chart

To convert metric measurements to imperial measurements, simply multiply the metric figure by the relevant number shown in the chart to the right. Bear in mind that conversions will not necessarily work out exactly, and you will need to round the figure up or down slightly. (Do not use a combination of metric and imperial measurements—for accuracy, always follow only one system.)

To convert	Multiply by
millimeters to inches	0.0394
meters to feet	3.28
meters to yards	1.093
sq. millimeters to sq. inches	0.00155
sq. meters to sq. feet	10.76
sq. meters to sq. yards	1.195
cu. meters to cu. feet	35.31
cu. meters to cu. yards	1.308
grams to pounds	0.0022
kilograms to pounds	2.2046
liters to gallons	0.22

Contents

Traditional
boardwalk
26

Decking
steps
30

Japanese
engawa
34

Circular
patio
38

Country
walkway
42

Japanese
bridge
46

Planter
containers
50

Checkerboard
decking patio
54

Decking area
with steps
58

Bench seat
and safety rail
62

Tree
ring seat
66

Adirondack
chair
70

Patio with
sandpit
76

Hillside
decking
82

Waterside
raised decking
88

Introduction

My brother's pied-à-terre in a Cornish seaside village is an exciting homage to wood—the walls are made from split oak, the roof is covered in wood, the front door is made from wood salvaged from a boatyard, and the stairs are made from walnut. But most impressively of all, the whole place is a wonderland of wooden decking. There is a small suspension bridge walkway from the gate to the first level, and raised decking jutting out from the house. The house backs onto the sea, and decking terraces lead down the cliff face to the beach, where a beautiful decking pier runs out to the sea. And so the idea for this book took off...

A brief history

There is some evidence that wooden walkways and platforms were built in ancient times, however decking as we know it today had its beginnings in such countries as Czechoslovakia, Germany, Poland, and Norway, and later in the pioneer towns in North America, Australia, and South Africa. In village and pioneer societies, where wood was abundant and time was short, the best way to construct walkways, porches, and platforms was to build them from rough-sawn lumber.

This beautiful covered porch in Rosedown, Louisiana, is complete with wooden baluster pillars, window shutters, and rocking chairs. Note the use of mixed-width decking boards.

Be inspired

The exciting thing about building decking is its immediacy. It might well be necessary to mix a small amount of concrete for the footings, but apart from that you can simply float the decking over an existing yard with all its problems (such as an old concrete patio that you just haven't got the energy to get rid of, a rocky outcrop that simply cannot be moved, or a patch of scrub). If you want to give your garden a swift makeover, take advantage of a splendid view, or simply expand your living space, this is the book for you.

Best of luck

The perfect place to spend a long, lazy afternoon—a stunning decking patio by a pool. The rugged, rough-sawn boards and the found posts look good in this setting.

Health and safety

Many woodworking procedures are potentially dangerous, so before starting work on the projects, check through the following list:

✔ Make sure that you are fit and strong enough for the task ahead of you. If you have doubts, ask your doctor for specific advice.

✔ Always use a ground-fault circuit interrupter (GFCI) between an electrical outlet and power tool (unless, of course, it's battery powered). Never use a power tool if the lawn is wet.

✔ If possible, use battery-powered tools instead of those with cables, because they are safer for outdoor projects.

✔ When you are lifting large weights from ground level, such as main posts and beams, minimize the risk of back strain by bending your knees, hugging the item close to your body, and keeping the spine upright.

✔ If items look too heavy to lift on your own, ask others to help. Don't risk injury.

✔ Wear a dust mask and goggles when using a power tool, such as a saber saw, and when sanding pressure-treated wood, because it is impregnated with a toxic preservative.

✔ Never operate a machine, such as a power drill, or attempt a difficult lifting or maneuvering task, if you are overtired or using medication.

✔ Keep a first-aid kit and telephone within easy reach.

✔ Allow children to watch at a safe distance and help with small tasks, but never leave them unsupervised.

Part 1
Techniques

Designing and planning

Decking is fun to build, but only if you spend time carefully designing and planning all the details of the project. It is vital to study the site, ask other family members for their views, consult neighbors if the intended construction could conceivably affect them, and draw up plans and list materials before you start ordering wood. This section explains what you need to know.

Looking at your outdoor space

Assessing your garden

Walk around the garden and consider your requirements for the decking. How do you want to use it? Will it be an area for sunbathing or for sitting in the shade? Do you want it for evening barbecues, or for the children to play on? Do you want the decking to be physically linked to the house, or set in isolation? Look at the levels of the land, note the position of the sun at different times of day and the prevailing direction of the wind, and observe the way the family usually moves around the yard. Think about possible sites.

Style considerations

Take into account the style of your house and its setting. You may decide that the decking should continue the theme of the house, and, for example, look folksy or modern. Alternatively, the decking could be a separate statement, providing a contrast to the style of the interior decor.

Split-level raised decking could well provide more living space

A Japanese bridge will give a new view of the pond

A decking seat around a favorite tree supplies a shaded spot to sit

A decking walkway will cover worn areas of grass surrounding the house

Whatever the size of your yard, there is a good chance that there is room for a decking feature—perhaps a patio or a decking bridge. Draw a plan of your yard and consider the possibilities, using several copies to sketch in various options.

Design

Shape, form, and structure

Once you have a clear idea of what you want to build, its site, and overall style, you need to work out the design in more detail. What shape do you want it to be? Do you want the decking to be raised high with feature stairs and decorative railings? Do the posts need to be set in concrete for stability? Does the decking have to wrap around the corner of the house, as for a Japanese engawa? Is the form so structurally complex that it will require a lot of bolts and braces? Will the decking incorporate existing features, such as trees and rocky outcrops?

Form and function

It is fine to allow form to dominate the design for a proposed project when it is no more than a plant container or small patio, but for other projects, safety reasons dictate that function must be the main consideration. For example, when you are building raised decking with steps and railings, or a chair that has to bear your weight and fold up for storage, function is much more important than form. The item has to be structurally sound and safe to use before pattern, texture, and color come into the picture.

Wood types

Always use the best wood that you can afford, especially when building more complex, time-consuming projects, such as a large area of decking. If money is no object, select long-lasting woods, such as redwood or oak. If you need to keep costs to a minimum, use pressure-treated pine. Either way, make sure that the wood is free from splits, twists, soft eroded edges, decay, dead knots, and insect infestation.

Drawing your designs

Phone three suppliers and ask about sizes and prices. Let's say, for example, that you need two 4-foot lengths of wood. The cheapest option might be for you to order a single 10-foot length and cut the wood to size yourself, instead of ordering two 4-foot lengths. If this is the case, there will be some wastage, therefore, would it be better to enlarge the project so that you use two 5-foot lengths?

Once you have made all the decisions regarding length and cost, sketch the design on paper—the plan view, front and side views, and the details. Include

the overall dimensions, the dimensions of the various sections, the number of pieces of wood, and any details concerning joints and fasteners. Make a list of the component parts—the number of lengths of each type of wood, and the number of bolts and fasteners required.

Before ordering wood and building, sit down in the yard with a piece of paper, inspirational pictures collected from magazines, and samples of decking materials. Spend some time considering the options. Design the project so that it suits all your needs.

Planning

First steps

Once you have ordered the wood, plan out the logistics of the project, from the moment the wood arrives to the actual order of work. Decide where you are going to stack the wood and whether you will need to buy more tools or sharpen old ones. If concrete is required, establish whether you will need to hire a cement mixer. If you are planning to work on a Sunday, find out if there is a nearby store where you can replenish supplies if, for example, you run out of screws. Is it feasible to complete the project in a single weekend, or would it be better to spread the work over two weekends? Will you have to wait for concrete to cure, or can you plan the tasks so that the concrete dries out overnight?

Permission and safety

Check with your local building department about any planning restrictions governing the type of structure you intend to build. Depending upon where you live, you might need permission before you can erect a "permanent structure." In some towns, you may be required to call your local building department to inspect footings before you continue to build your decking.

Follow proper safety procedures and wear gloves to guard your hands against splinters and abrasion, goggles to protect your eyes, and strong boots to stop your feet being crushed. Always wear a dust mask when sanding pressure-treated wood or wood that has been brushed with a preservative.

Planning checklist

✔ Are there any mills in your area? These will be the most economical source of materials.

✔ Can you save money by modifying the projects to suit a particular size or type of wood?

✔ Are local suppliers willing to deliver small quantities of wood?

✔ Is there adequate access to your yard, with a wide entrance and possibly room for a truck to turn?

✔ If the wood is unloaded in your driveway or front yard, will it cause problems or pose a danger?

✔ How are you going to move the wood from the driveway to the site? Will you need friends to help?

Materials

The only reliable way to get top-quality wood is to go to the lumberyard and choose it yourself, instead of ordering it unseen. First, make phone calls to find the best quotes, then arm yourself with a detailed list of your needs—types of wood, quantity, and the various lengths and sections—and visit the supplier to examine the wood available. Choose the boards yourself, one by one. The following section shows you how.

Using lumber and other decking materials

Width, thickness, and length

Lumberyards sell wood that is termed "rough" and "surfaced." Rough-sawn wood comes as cut at the mill, while surfaced wood has been planed smooth. Wood is sold in "nominal sizes," which is the size of the wood when first cut. However, what you buy will be smaller—wood shrinks slightly after being cut, and it may have been planed. Softwood loses $\frac{1}{2}$ inch in each dimension, for example a 2 x 4 is actually $1\frac{1}{2}$ x $3\frac{1}{2}$. Hardwood loses about $\frac{1}{4}$ inch in thickness and is sold with the thickness given in fractions—for example, "5/4" is a nominal $1\frac{1}{4}$ inch.

Lumber types and textures

Wood is sold in various grades—the higher the grade the better the wood. Some lumberyards offer a variety of top-quality wood species, such as redwood, cedar, and oak, which are long-lasting and resistant to rot and insect attack. Lumberyards also sell less-expensive pine that has been pressure-treated with either brown or green chemical preservatives.

We favor using rough-sawn wood for the projects, which we swiftly sand to remove splinters, then protect and color with washes of exterior masonry paint, or with a traditional lime wash.

Other materials

Plastic ground sheeting; gravel and crushed stone; aggregate, sand, and cement; and all types of screws, nails, and bolts are used in the projects. Gravel and crushed stone are used as decorative spreads and as a drainage bed, and aggregate (a mixture of sand and gravel) is used when making concrete. When selecting nails, screws, and bolts, opt for plated or galvanized types. We prefer to use screws instead of nails, because they have more holding power. Bolts are good when you need an extra-strong joint, such as when fitting joists to posts, or building frames.

Buying wood

Take a tape measure and hand-pick every board and post on your list. Don't be intimidated. Reject wood that is split, twisted, or in any way less than perfect.

Caution
Pressure-treated lumber
Wear gloves when handling newly treated wood, and avoid contact with the sawdust. Wash your hands before eating or drinking.

Opposite page: A selection of materials suitable for making the projects in this book. 1 Gravel, 2 Plastic ground sheeting, 3 "Fence capping," 4 Preserved decking, 5 Pressure-treated decking, 6 Grooved decking, 7 Wide decking board, 8 Standard screws, 9 Deck screws, 10 Untreated decking, 11 Acorn finial, 12 Standard nails, 13 Carriage bolt, 14 Joist, 15 Post, 16 Round-section post, 17 Wood chips.

Concrete and other post-securing materials

Most decking has to be set on some type of foundation.

- For a small area of low-level decking: dig post holes, set posts on 4 in. of gravel, and fill holes with gravel.

- For decking on solid ground: place precast concrete piers on the ground, set the posts directly in position.

- For damp, compacted soil: dig post holes, add 4 in. of gravel, insert posts, fill with dryish concrete mix.

- For sandy soil or frost-prone areas, with the footing extended above ground level: dig post holes, set a fiberboard tube or form in the holes so that the top is at the desired level, put 4 in. of gravel into the tube and top it with concrete. Push a post anchor into the wet concrete, or paint the bottom of a concrete pier with a concrete bonding agent and set it 1–2 in. in concrete.

Caution
Cement and lime are both corrosive. Always wear a dust mask, gloves, and goggles. If you do get the powder on your skin, especially if your skin is damp, wash it off immediately using plenty of water.

Tools

Tools are one of the main keys to successful woodwork. A few carefully chosen, medium-priced tools will make every task a pleasure to complete. But to save on costs, avoid splashing out on a complete new set of tools, and start out by using the tools that you already have at hand. Buy new tools when you really need them. Here is a list of tools which, in an ideal world, would reside in your tool kit.

Useful tools for building decking

Tools for preparing the site

You will need a large fibreglass tape measure for measuring the site, wooden pegs and string for setting the limits of the decking, and a club hammer for banging in pegs. You will also require a spade for cutting away turf and digging holes, and a bucket, wheelbarrow, shovel, and rake for all the soil-moving tasks. Choose tools to suit your strength and height—for example, you can buy different sizes of spades and sledgehammers. A spirit level is needed for checking levels, both on the decking and when setting out pegs.

Measuring and marking

A small tape measure is used for measuring lengths and widths, a square for drawing and checking right angles, and a compass or a pair of dividers for drawing circle-based curves.

A handful of good, strong carpenter's pencils is vital—they last longer than ordinary pencils, and they don't roll off the workbench. If you are making decking with angles greater or smaller than 90 degrees, you will also need a bevel gauge or an engineer's protractor square.

Sawing wood

A couple of handsaws are always useful. We use a crosscut saw for cutting wood to length across the grain, and a rip saw for cutting a board down its length.

When it comes to cutting curves, we use an electric saber saw. Occasionally, we use a hand coping saw for cutting tight curves and little details. If you particularly enjoy using power tools, consider obtaining a small combination miter saw, which is a really good tool for making a large number of identical cuts.

Drilling and screwing

We use a straightforward power drill for drilling deep, large-diameter holes, and a cordless drill in conjunction with a crosshead screwdriver bit for driving in screws. However, if the weather is damp, or we are too lazy to unroll the cable for the power drill, we might use the cordless drill both for drilling holes and driving in screws. If, by the end of the day, the cordless drill has run out of power, we might also use the power drill to drive in screws. If you intend to build a lot of decking, it's a good idea to invest in two cordless drills, so that you can always have one charging in readiness.

Nailing

Before nailing, you will need one of the drills to drill pilot holes, then a claw hammer to knock in the nails. If the workpiece needs to be supported, to stop it shaking or bouncing, hold a sledgehammer or a club hammer at the back of it. We generally have at least two or three claw hammers on site, so that there is always one near at hand—on the ground, on the decking, somewhere on the woodpile, or on the workbench.

Holding and securing

Ideally, you need two portable workbenches so that you can cut long lengths of wood comfortably, without asking for help. We use two inexpensive benches, so we don't worry about giving them a lot of rough treatment. If you are trying to cut costs, you could even work on a couple of old wooden chests. If you are doing most of the work on your own, you will also need a couple of large-size clamps for holding the workpiece in place while you are drilling holes and screwing. It is important to keep your back straight while you work, to avoid strain.

Tool hire

If your main interest is in the end results of a particular project instead of in taking up woodwork and decking construction as a future hobby, it might be better to borrow the larger and more expensive tools. If you need a large sander or a cement mixer, the most sensible course of action is to hire the piece of equipment.

Caution
Power tools

Electricity, early-morning dew, buckets of water, and wet hands are a potentially dangerous combination. If you use a power drill, electric cement mixer, or other power tool, make sure that you use it with a ground-fault circuit interrupter (GFCI) to prevent an electric shock.

A basic tool kit

For making the projects in this book, you will need to buy or borrow the tools shown below. All these basic, everyday tools can be bought from a home center or hardware store. Larger pieces of equipment can be hired. Items that are not illustrated include a portable workbench, wheelbarrow, and bucket (the last two are for making concrete, which may be necessary for securing posts in the ground to support areas of decking).

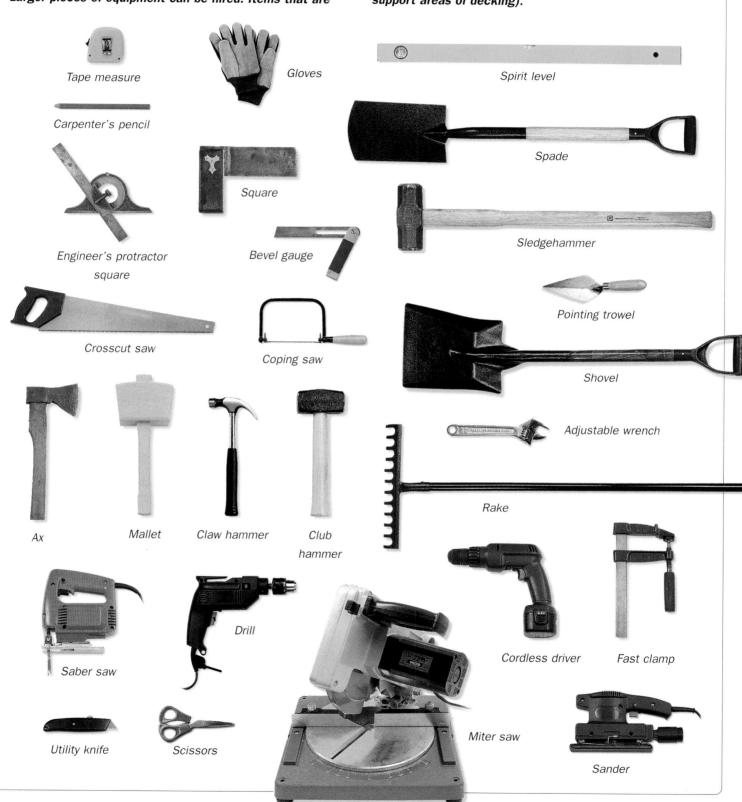

Tape measure

Gloves

Spirit level

Carpenter's pencil

Square

Spade

Engineer's protractor square

Bevel gauge

Sledgehammer

Crosscut saw

Coping saw

Pointing trowel

Shovel

Ax

Mallet

Claw hammer

Club hammer

Adjustable wrench

Rake

Saber saw

Drill

Cordless driver

Fast clamp

Utility knife

Scissors

Miter saw

Sander

Basic techniques

Once you have a clear understanding of the basic techniques, and you can handle the tools with confidence, building decking is an enjoyable experience. The secret is to work at an easy, comfortable pace, and not to rush things. Make sure you spend plenty of time assessing the intended site to ensure that it is suitable, measure accurately, and always double-check before you make a cut.

Marking out

Securing the position of the posts

Once you have decided where you want to build the decking, establish the positions of the levels of decking and all the holes for the supporting posts. Secure a reference post in position and at the correct height, then use pegs, string, and the crossed diagonal method to relate all the other posts and levels to this point. We usually set the reference post on the high point of the site. The crossed diagonal method involves measuring each of the diagonals of a given rectangle (such as a marked-out site, or an area of decking), and ensuring that they are the same. If not, adjustments are made until they are.

Check that the diagonal measurements of the rectangle are identical

Check that the lengths of the rectangle's sides are equal

Due to the large scale of decking projects, it is often difficult to tell by eye alone if a rectangular structure—such as a decking frame—is square (has 90° corners). You will need to use a tape measure to check the length, width, and diagonal measurements.

Initial tasks

Preparing the site

Once you have worked out the precise position of the post holes, you will need to think about the existing foliage (lawn and plants) that is growing on the area that will be covered by the decking.

There is no problem if the decking is going to be high enough off the ground to walk under, but if it will be at a low level, remove the turf, roughly level the ground and lay a plastic ground sheet over it, then cover the plastic with gravel. This system not only controls the weeds, but it also allows rainwater to drain away freely. If the decking is going to be positioned just clear of the ground, all you need do is level out the bumps, lay down

a piece of plastic ground sheet, then simply rest the decking directly on short piles or concrete piers, so the joists are not in contact with the soil.

Setting posts in the ground

Dig a hole down to firm ground, or to the depth required by your local building department. It needs to be twice as big as the post. Shovel about 4 inches of gravel into the hole, and set the post in position. Pour in concrete to surround the post, filling the hole to ground level. Tamp the concrete with a beam to release air bubbles, check that the post is upright with a spirit level, then secure it in place temporarily, bracing it with lengths of 1 x 2s.

Carriage bolts are used to fasten a load-bearing joist to a post

Concrete is troweled to a smooth finish to repel water

The decking frame (the main posts and joists) must be square, level, and well secured. Concrete secures the posts into the ground, so they do not move.

Cutting lumber to size

Cutting across the grain

A power saw is one option for cutting across the grain, but if you are a beginner it is best to use a new crosscut saw. Mark the line of cut with the square and pencil, and support the workpiece on the workbench. Place the saw to the waste side of the mark, draw the blade toward you to start the cut, then continue sawing. When the saw is three-parts through the wood, hook your free hand around to support the waste, and complete the cut. A compound miter saw is very useful when you need to repeat a large number of angled cuts, such as for laying decking at an angle to the frame.

Cutting curves

A saber saw is a great tool for making curved cuts in wood up to about 2 inches thick. To use it, set the blade on the mark, switch on the power, and slowly advance along the waste side of the drawn line. To avoid dangerous kickbacks, always switch off the power before you remove the tool from the workpiece.

Use an inexpensive, portable workbench to hold and support the workpiece. If you want, use a clamp to grasp the work firmly.

Joints

Jointing with screws

There are various decking clips, fasteners, and brackets on the market, but they are not the strongest, most attractive, or even the swiftest option. Also, many beginners find these fasteners both expensive and confusing. For these reasons, we have opted for traditional joints held together either with cross-head screws or with carriage bolts. Occasionally, we use nails, but screws have more holding power and can be driven in or removed without damaging the wood. The order of work is to first drill a pilot hole, set the screw in place, and drive it in with the cordless drill fitted with a cross-head screwdriver bit. If you are working with a partner, with one of you drilling the holes and the other driving in the screws, this technique can be just as fast as nailing.

Jointing with bolts

When an extra-strong joint is required, such as for fastening main joists to main posts, it is best to use a bolt. You can use a machine bolt with a washer at each end, or a carriage bolt with a domed head and a square shoulder between the head and the shank. We prefer carriage bolts, not only because the round head is more attractive, but they can also be fitted using a single wrench.

A cordless driver is the best tool for putting in screws

When you are laying boards on a large structure, always stagger the joints, because this gives the best effect visually.

Washers are always used with carriage-bolted joints, along with a socket wrench or adjustable wrench to tighten the nuts.

Finishing

Finishing

From the moment that your decking is completed, it will be subject to attack by the sun, rain, and insects, so the wood needs to be protected. Traditionally, decking was limewashed or even tarred. There are many finishes on the market, from oils and resins to preservatives and varnishes. We generally prefer to start off with pressure-treated wood, and finish it with a coat of color. So we might mix lime with water, or thin down exterior-grade masonry paint until we have a wash. The resulting surface looks weathered and blends in with the yard.

Walkways and patios

Wooden decking walkways and patios look delightful and provide dry, level areas for safe and comfortable walking. They also attract your attention—the moment you see Japanese engawa decking running out of sight around the corner of a house, or a decking patio complete with a chair, you will be drawn to go and have a closer look. So for a striking, practical addition to your yard, opt for decking.

Constructing walkways

Designing and planning

Walk around your garden and decide precisely where you want the walkway to be sited. Take note of the levels of the land, because these will have to be accommodated, and consider how the walkway will impact on your use of the garden.

Decide on the details of the decking's structure—the height off the ground and the position of the main beams—and use a tape measure, pegs, and string to map out the site accordingly.

Building

Remove all large plants, level the ground, and dig out roots and large stones. To prevent weeds, spread a layer of plastic ground sheeting over the entire site, and cover it with a generous layer of gravel. The wetter the site, the deeper the gravel needs to be to ensure stability. Position the pressure-treated beams on the gravel and screw the decking boards in place.

A simple walkway that turns into a basic bridge complements the restrained planting scheme of this garden. The decking is supported on a concrete base and edged with split logs. The concrete supports for the three-board bridge are concealed behind the stacked slate walls.

INSPIRATIONS

A curving decking walkway, edged with cobblestones, looks beautiful alongside a pond.

Decking boards lend themselves to crisp, geometrical layouts.

A walkway and water crossing built from treated wood make an attractive feature.

Constructing a patio

Designing and planning

Think about how your garden looks over all the seasons, then, in the light of your observations about sunshine, shade, being overlooked by neighbors, and so on, decide on the best place for siting the patio. Use a tape measure, pegs, and string to mark out the boundaries of the site.

Building

If your garden is reasonably dry and level, and you want the patio close to the ground instead of raised, you can use the same techniques used for building walkways, and set the patio on a plastic ground sheet and gravel. Decking walkways tend to consist of two tracks that run in straight or slightly curved lines, with decking boards bridging the tracks, but a patio offers you the opportunity to build a form that is both shapely and patterned. Once the plastic and gravel are in place, mark out the outer profile of the decking and divide it with a pattern of joists set 12–18 inches apart at their centers. Make sure that the pattern of joists relates to the planned layout or pattern of your decking, so that there is plenty of support for the ends of the boards.

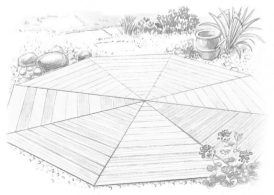

This patio and walkway uses a mixture of straight and wedge-shaped boards. The decking is laid on gravel and set at the same depth as the lawn for easy mowing.

This generously sized ground-level decking looks ideally suited to the country house setting (New Orleans, Louisiana). The owners needed a large seating area for barbecues and family gatherings. They wanted the patio to complement the existing tree, which offers shade. The key to this type of decking patio is establishing a firm, level base (a low-lying frame).

A simple layout of decking tiles is perfectly suited to a small yard, balcony, or courtyard.

An octagonal patio is attention-grabbing. It is also easier to build than a circular patio.

A walkway along a well-trodden route between house and garden is a prime site for decking.

Decking

Decking can invigorate a family's use of their outdoor space, allowing many more activities to take place there. The space can be transformed by an area of raised decking standing high above the garden, or a subtle Japanese engawa running around the house, or even an island decking. Decking is also a crafty way of making a difficult-to-use area, such as a bank, participate fully in the life of the yard.

Constructing an engawa

Designing and planning

In a traditional Japanese garden, an *engawa* is a strip of low-level wooden decking that encircles the house, linking it to the yard. If you like the idea of having your own, walk around your house and have a good look at the levels of the land. Is it possible for an engawa to have a free passage around the house, or will it have to bridge immovable obstacles, such as downspouts and splash blocks? If you have to bridge them, make sure that your decking includes inspection hatches. If there are existing walkways, steps, and trees, decide whether to leave them in place and run the decking over or around them, or whether to remove them. Use a tape measure, pegs, and string to mark out the route of the engawa.

Building

Mark out the position of the footings at no more than 6 feet apart, dig holes, and concrete short stub posts into place. Cover the site with plastic, topped with gravel. Bridge the posts with beams and link the beams with joists. Bridge the beams with decking boards.

This Japanese teahouse in southern California has an engawa walkway. The lumber decking is minimal and practical, echoing the design of the building.

INSPIRATIONS

Stepped decking with an integral bench and railing, and under-seat storage space.

Low-level decking is ideal for a pond-side patio. A tree has been incorporated for shade.

Raised decking with steps and a handrail. The trellis screens off the neighboring garden.

Island decking

This simple island decking includes an integral bench seat. The wood has been limewashed to create a cool, weathered effect (a welcome change to the popular red-brown finishes).

Island decking can be built just about anywhere in the garden, so you can site it to take advantage of views, morning sun, afternoon shade, or whatever you desire. Use a tape measure, pegs, and string to mark out the location of the footings. Dig holes and concrete the posts in position. Screw the main beams to the posts, make adjustments to correct the levels, and bolt the beams in place. Trim the tops off the posts, set joists on the beams, and lay the decking as already described.

Raised decking with steps

Raised decking with steps is a great option for a home that is several steps above ground level, where there is a need to build decking that is close to the house but not actually attached to it.

Use a tape measure, pegs, and string to establish the position of the footings and to mark out the total plan area. Concrete the posts into the ground. The secret of building decking of this type is to start by bolting a registration or ledger beam as close as possible to the house, then use it as a marker for all the other levels.

The owners of this raised decking with steps, in New Orleans, Louisiana, had to deal with the problem of varying ground levels in their yard. The ideal solution was to lay decking to cover the entire area.

A decking porch with steps and railing provides an area for walking and sitting.

This porch walkway with a handrail uses trellis to cover the gap underneath.

Traditional raised decking overlooking the sea makes a perfect area for relaxation.

Decking additions

Once the decking is in place, such additions as railings, steps, and benches offer you an opportunity for artistic expression in terms of pattern and form. If you like Japanese lattice screens, Swiss cottage fretwork, bold modernism or American folk colors, now is the time to incorporate them into your design. For sources of inspiration, have a look through the interior decor and architecture sections in a bookstore or library.

Constructing steps

This multilevel decking in Louisiana incorporates bench seating. Steps are an obvious requirement for sloping sites and can be the most challenging aspect of the whole job of design and construction. Broad steps are more people-friendly than narrow stairways.

Designing and planning

Look at the site and use a tape measure, lengths of 1 x 2s, and pencil to establish the total distance along the ground that the flight of steps will cover, and the total height from one level to another. Decide on the riser height (4–7 inches), divide the total height by this number, and minus one to give the number of risers. Divide the horizontal distance along the ground by the number of risers to obtain the maximum depth of the treads.

Building

For the stringers (sides of the steps), choose between zigzag stringers or solid planks. Start by measuring and cutting the two stringers so that they run parallel to each other, with their feet on the ground and their heads firmly secured to the edge of the decking. Once the stringers are in place, the rest is easy. A simple box platform doesn't need stringers.

INSPIRATIONS

This delightfully simple bridge or walkway draws inspiration from Japanese gardens.

Built-in seating with railings and planters, following a symmetrical arrangement.

Two planters bridged with boards provide a simple seat. A backrest is optional.

Railings

Ask your local building department for advice and information about railing height, the recommended distance apart for the main posts, and other safety factors. The primary concern is that children cannot get their heads stuck between rails, or slip between the decking and the bottom horizontal rail. Consider your particular needs. Do the railings need to be especially safe because the decking is high off the ground, or are they more of a privacy screen or a windbreak? The order of work is to bolt the main posts in place, top them with the banister rail, then fit the baluster rails or screen. The balusters afford you the opportunity to build in decorative details.

Benches

Look at the seating in your house in order to decide on the height and depth for a bench (seats are likely to be about 16 inches above the ground). A bench can be secured as part of the railings around the decking, or it can be free-standing so you can move it around. If a railing also forms the back of the bench, remember that children might climb on the bench, so the railing will need to be made higher. Once you have worked out the height of the seat, and the height and angle of the backrest, the actual building is very straightforward.

High railings are combined with a lattice screen. The owners wanted to make sure that the raised decking was safe for their small children and pets to use.

A beautifully crafted bench makes this wonderful roofed decking even more enticing. Imagine sitting there and soaking up the view after a hard day's work.

A bench built around a tree is a great place to sit—perfect for escaping from the sun.

What better way of enjoying decking than to stretch out on a home-made sun lounger?

A traditional American Adirondack chair is just the thing for a decking porch.

Part 2
Projects

Traditional boardwalk

There is something very special about a traditional decking boardwalk—it looks spectacular in its simplicity and feels good underfoot. The act of walking on the boards produces a characteristic drumming that will remind you of a seaside pier. This project is for the simplest type of boardwalk—a straight walkway—but you can design one that turns corners, follows a curve, or changes level.

★
Easy

**Making time
One weekend**
One day for putting the beams in place, and one day for fitting and securing the decking

Considering the design

The traditional boardwalk is very simple in construction—just two lines of posts that are banged directly into the ground, with beams lapped onto the posts to make two parallel rails. These are topped with weathered, rough-sawn decking. The tops of the 4-inch-square posts stand about 6 inches clear of the ground, allowing the boardwalk to skim over uneven land. This walkway is quick and easy to build, and it is suitable for various situations, such as over a lawn or through a wood setting.

Getting started

Study your site and decide on the route of the boardwalk. Look at the ground and make checks with the spirit level to establish how far above ground level the decking needs to be. Your requirements may be different to the specifications of the project (6¾ inches above ground level); for example, there may be boulders protruding from the ground that you would be easier to build over instead of digging out, or the ground may be uneven and undulating.

Measure the length of the proposed boardwalk from one end to the other to calculate the wood required. We have quoted quantities per 6½-foot length of boardwalk. Order the wood and, when it is delivered, stack it as close as possible to the site. Set out your workbenches and tools, and you are ready to begin.

Overall dimensions and general notes

The surface of the decking is 6¾ in. above the ground

3 ft. wide

A traditional boardwalk will look good in just about any garden. It can be painted or left a natural color.

You will need

Tools

- ✔ Two portable workbenches
- ✔ Pencil, ruler, tape measure, and square
- ✔ Crosscut saw
- ✔ Wooden mallet
- ✔ Small hand ax
- ✔ Pegs and string
- ✔ Spade
- ✔ Sledgehammer
- ✔ Spirit level
- ✔ Cordless power drill with a cross-head screwdriver bit
- ✔ Drill bit to match the size of the screws
- ✔ Two ¼-in.-thick scrap pieces of sawn wood or plywood, to use as spacers

Materials

(All rough-sawn pieces of pine include excess length for wastage. All the wood is pressure-treated with preservative.)

For approximately 6 ft. 6 in. of boardwalk, 3 ft. wide

- ✔ Pine: 1 rough-sawn 4 x 4, 10 ft. long (posts)
- ✔ Pine: 2 rough-sawn 2 x 4s, 6 ft. 6 in. long (beams)
- ✔ Pine: 10 rough-sawn 1 x 4s, 6 ft. 6 in. long (decking boards)
- ✔ Zinc-plated, countersunk cross-head screws: 100 x 3½-in.-long no. 10

Exploded view of the traditional boardwalk

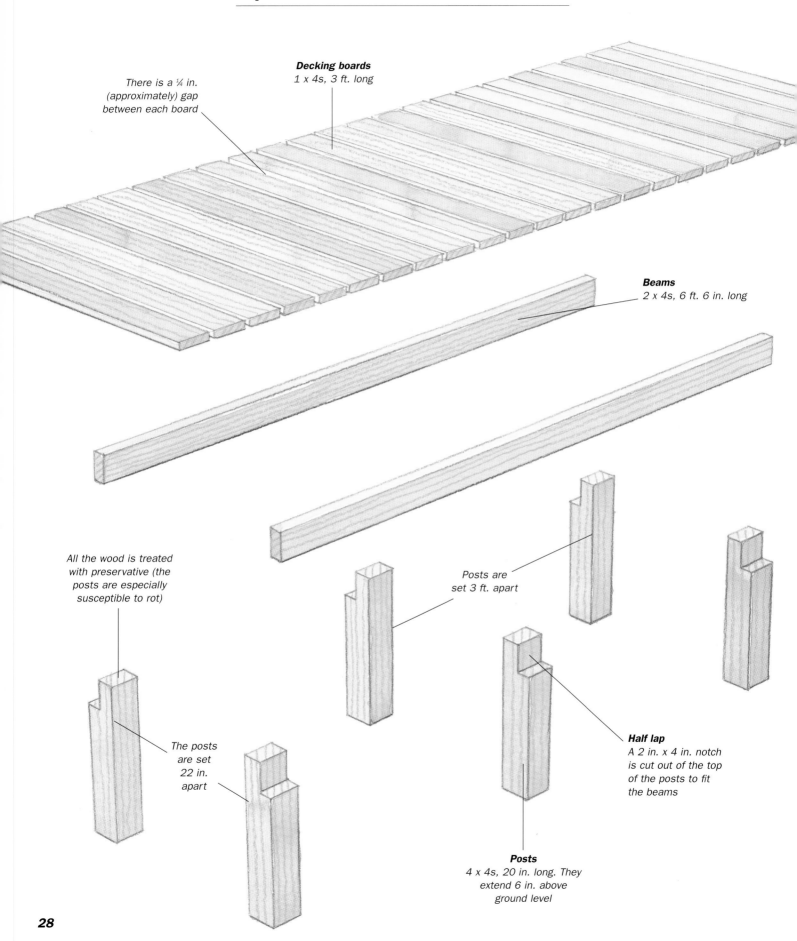

Decking boards
1 x 4s, 3 ft. long

There is a ¼ in. (approximately) gap between each board

Beams
2 x 4s, 6 ft. 6 in. long

All the wood is treated with preservative (the posts are especially susceptible to rot)

Posts are set 3 ft. apart

The posts are set 22 in. apart

Half lap
A 2 in. x 4 in. notch is cut out of the top of the posts to fit the beams

Posts
4 x 4s, 20 in. long. They extend 6 in. above ground level

Making the traditional boardwalk

1 Cutting the posts
Saw the 4 x 4 posts into 20 in. lengths, and use the ruler and square to lay out 2 in. x 4 in. half lap joints. Saw across the grain to establish the length of the lap, then use the mallet and ax to clear the waste.

2 Positioning the posts
Use the tape measure, pegs, string, spade, and sledgehammer to set the posts in the ground. Place the centers of the posts 22 in. apart across the width and 3 ft. apart along the length of the boardwalk. They all extend 6 in. above the ground.

3 Fastening the beams
Set the beams for supporting the decking in position. Lay them on the half laps in the posts, and fasten them in place with 3½ in.-long screws. (When fastening the beams end to end like this, make sure that they meet at the center of the posts.)

4 Laying the decking
Cut the 4 x 4 decking boards into 3 ft. lengths, and screw them in place across the beams. Center the boards on the beams and use the ¼-in.-thick scrap wood to space them apart.

Decking steps

All too often, steps are not built to take account of the people who use them, and they are difficult to negotiate for anyone using a walking cane or stroller. If you want to make a grand and easy entrance, decking steps are the perfect answer— and the great advantage of this project is that they can be built over existing steps to just about any size that you desire.

★
Easy

Making time
One day
Two hours for planning and measuring, and the rest of the time for the woodwork

Considering the design

The decking steps fit over your existing steps in such a way that, although they hardly change the height of the riser, they greatly increase the available standing area. You will, of course, have to modify the design to suit your particular steps, but we have made the design very flexible, so that it is easy to change.

Consider the attractions of the project. Perhaps you have an elderly relation who is unsteady on her feet and would like to be able to stand squarely on one very large step before moving to another.

Or you might simply want to give your steps a makeover to give them a more generous and inviting feel, or provide a place for container plants by the door.

Getting started

Study the design, then carefully measure your existing steps and see how the design needs to be altered to fit them. The project is for a two-step unit, but you might have to change to a one- or three-step unit. Check whether you need to make changes to the wood sizes, or perhaps to the overall dimensions.

You will need

Tools

- ✔ Two portable workbenches
- ✔ Pencil, ruler, tape measure, marking gauge, and square
- ✔ Crosscut saw
- ✔ Cordless power drill with a cross-head screwdriver bit
- ✔ Drill bits to match the sizes of the screws
- ✔ Spirit level
- ✔ Sander

Materials

(All rough-sawn pieces of pine include excess length for wastage. All the wood is pressure-treated with preservative.)

For steps 6 ft. 6 in. wide and 4 ft. deep

- ✔ Pine: 8 rough-sawn 2 x 4s, 6 ft. 6 in. long (joists)
- ✔ Pine: 2 rough-sawn 3 x 3s, 6 ft. 6 in. long (main vertical supports)
- ✔ Pine: 20 rough-sawn 1 x 4s, 6 ft. 6 in. long (decking and riser boards)
- ✔ Zinc-plated, countersunk cross-head screws: 100 x 3-in.-long no. 8, 200 x 2-in.-long no. 8

Overall dimensions and general notes

The project is a good way of improving an existing doorstep that you consider to be too narrow or unattractive. The decking steps are built over the top of the existing steps.

The length, width, and height can be adjusted to suit the existing steps

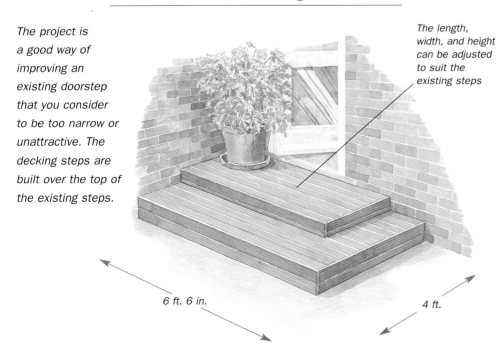

6 ft. 6 in.

4 ft.

Exploded view of the decking steps

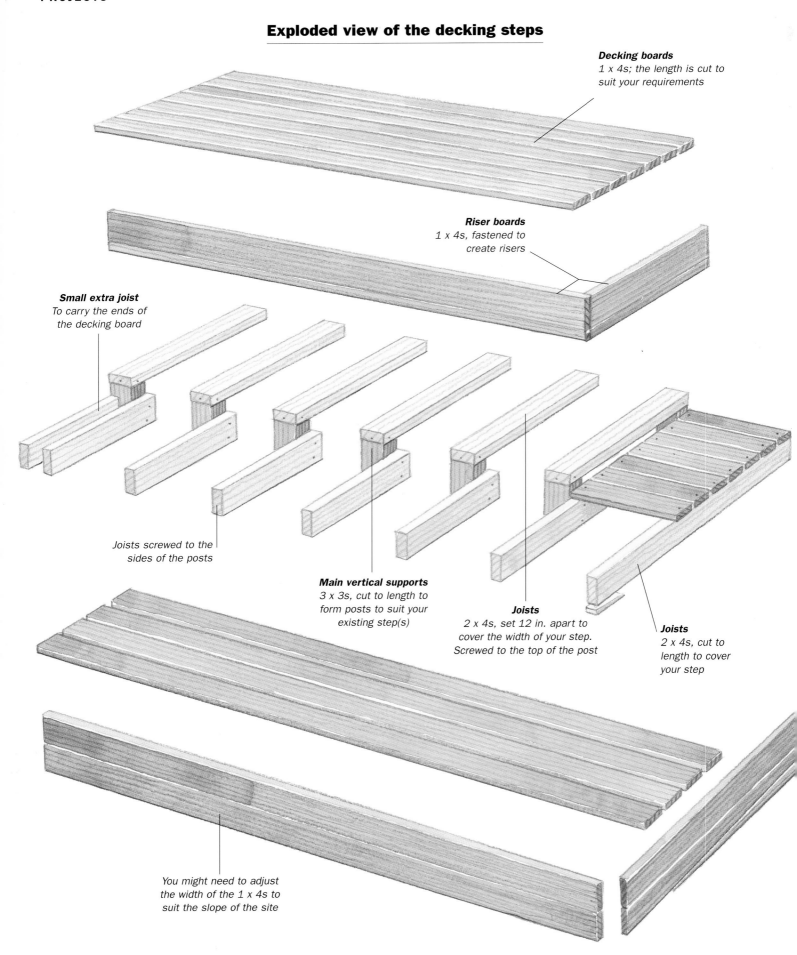

Decking boards
1 x 4s; the length is cut to
suit your requirements

Riser boards
1 x 4s, fastened to
create risers

Small extra joist
To carry the ends of
the decking board

Joists screwed to the
sides of the posts

Main vertical supports
3 x 3s, cut to length to
form posts to suit your
existing step(s)

Joists
2 x 4s, set 12 in. apart to
cover the width of your step.
Screwed to the top of the post

Joists
2 x 4s, cut to
length to cover
your step

You might need to adjust
the width of the 1 x 4s to
suit the slope of the site

Making the decking steps

1 Fastening the joists
Measure your existing set of steps from front to back, and cut the joists to length accordingly. Set the joists 12 in. apart (to match the full front to back measurement of your steps), and hold them in place with two lengths of decking. Fasten with 2-in.-long screws.

2 Siting the frame
Place the joist frame over your steps, and level it with scrap wood or whatever is at hand. Use a spirit level to check the levels in all directions.

3 Fastening the vertical supports
Cut main vertical supports from the 3 x 3s. With 3-in.-long screws, fasten them under the ends of the joists, so each joist has its own support.

4 Building the bottom step
Repeat the procedure already described to build a frame for the bottom step. Set the step at the correct level and cut each main vertical support to suit the level of the ground.

5 Fitting the decking
When the frames for the two steps are in place, cover them with the decking boards, using 2-in.-long screws. When you come to fitting the riser boards on the bottom step, you will almost certainly have to adjust the width of the board along its length, tapering it to suit the run of the ground. Finally, sand the steps.

Japanese engawa

In a traditional Japanese yard, an *engawa* is low-level wooden decking that encircles the house, linking it to the yard and blurring the boundaries between the two. The engawa is made up of three component parts: a walkway that runs along the side of the building, a raised decking corner unit that sits at the corner of the building, and a set of steps that runs from the corner unit down to the ground.

Making time
One weekend
One day for making the basic frame; one day for fastening boards and making the steps

Considering the design

By using combinations of these three basic units, you can design a scheme to suit your own requirements.

Getting started

Decide how many units you will need. The details for the steps are in the project Decking Area with Steps (page 58). Measure the total length of your walkway, and divide it into the 8-foot-long modules for which we have given quantities.

Overall dimensions and general notes

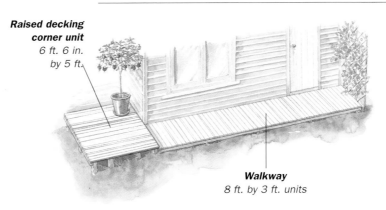

Raised decking corner unit
6 ft. 6 in. by 5 ft.

Walkway
8 ft. by 3 ft. units

Using a combination of straight walkways and raised corner units, the engawa can be adapted to suit your situation.

You will need

Tools

- Pencil, ruler, tape measure, and square
- Pegs and string
- Two portable workbenches
- Crosscut saw
- Cordless power drill with a cross-head screwdriver bit
- Drill bits to match the sizes of the screws
- Utility knife
- Staple gun
- Spade and shovel
- Wheelbarrow and bucket
- Spirit level
- Sander
- Paintbrush

Materials

(All rough-sawn pieces of pine include excess length for wastage. All the wood is pressure-treated with preservative.)

For each 8-ft. length of walkway

- Pine: 3 rough-sawn 2 x 4s, 10 ft. long (joists)
- Pine: 1 rough-sawn 3 x 3, 10 ft. long (posts)
- Pine: 8 rough-sawn 1 x 4s, 10 ft. long (decking boards)
- Pine: 3 rough-sawn 1 x 2s, 10 ft. long (decking boards)

For each 6-ft.-6-in.- by 5-ft. corner unit

- Pine: 4 rough-sawn 2 x 4s, 6 ft. 6 in. long (joists)
- Pine: 4 rough-sawn 3 x 3s, 6 ft. 6 in. long (posts)
- Pine: 7 rough-sawn 1 x 4s, 10 ft. long, (decking boards)

- Pine: 1 rough-sawn 1 x 10, 10 ft. long (decking boards)
- Pine: 3 rough-sawn 1 x 2s, 10 ft. long (decking boards)

General

- Zinc-plated, countersunk cross-head screws: 200 x 3-in.-long no. 8, 100 x 3½-in.-long no. 10
- Galvanized staples: 100 x ⅜ in. wide
- Concrete: 1 part (44 lb.) Portland cement, 5 parts (220 lb.) aggregate (for every 9 posts)
- Plastic ground sheet (large enough for the total decking area of the ground-level walkways)
- Exterior-grade matte white paint

Exploded view of the Japanese engawa

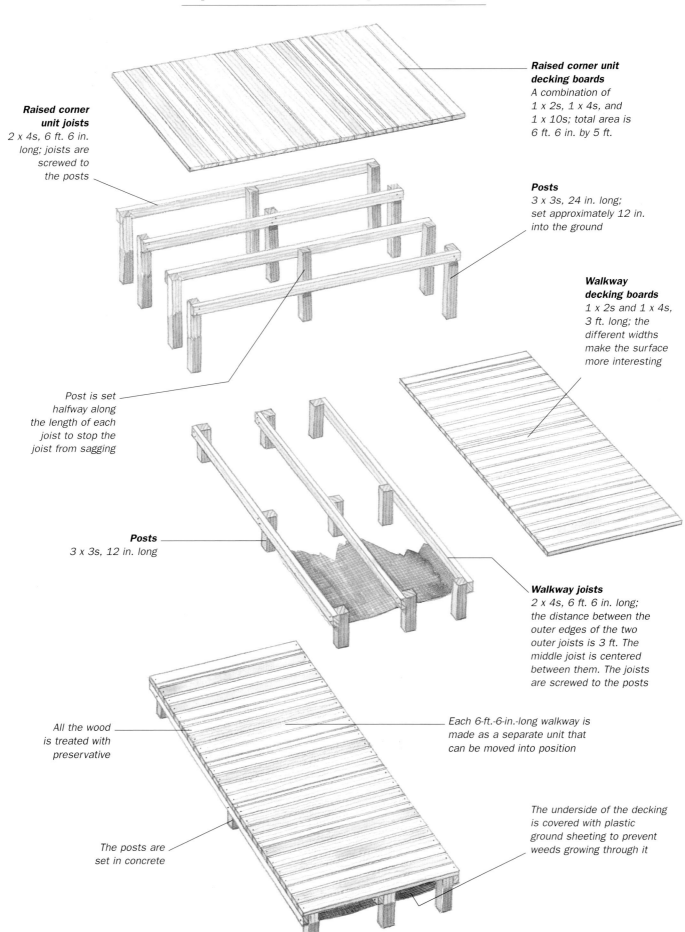

Raised corner unit decking boards
A combination of 1 x 2s, 1 x 4s, and 1 x 10s; total area is 6 ft. 6 in. by 5 ft.

Raised corner unit joists
2 x 4s, 6 ft. 6 in. long; joists are screwed to the posts

Posts
3 x 3s, 24 in. long; set approximately 12 in. into the ground

Walkway decking boards
1 x 2s and 1 x 4s, 3 ft. long; the different widths make the surface more interesting

Post is set halfway along the length of each joist to stop the joist from sagging

Posts
3 x 3s, 12 in. long

Walkway joists
2 x 4s, 6 ft. 6 in. long; the distance between the outer edges of the two outer joists is 3 ft. The middle joist is centered between them. The joists are screwed to the posts

All the wood is treated with preservative

Each 6-ft.-6-in.-long walkway is made as a separate unit that can be moved into position

The posts are set in concrete

The underside of the decking is covered with plastic ground sheeting to prevent weeds growing through it

Making the Japanese engawa

1 Building the walkway frame
Take three 6-ft.-6-in. lengths of wood for the joists, and position them as shown on the drawing to make the basic three-joist frame. Screw a 3-ft.-long piece of 1-in.-thick decking board at each end to hold the frame square, using 3-in.-long screws.

2 Fastening the plastic
Turn the frame upside-down, and cut a piece of the plastic ground sheet to fit. Staple it to what will be the underside of the joists.

3 Screwing on the posts
Cut nine 12-in. lengths of 3 x 3, and screw them to the joists with $3\frac{1}{2}$-in.-long screws to make the posts (cut the plastic to fit around each post). Put one at each end of the joists, and one halfway along their length to provide a central support.

4 Concreting the posts
Set the frame on the ground and establish the position of the posts. Dig holes $8\frac{1}{4}$ in. deep. (The walkway sits at ground level.) Make a dryish mix of concrete, put it in the holes, and lower the frame into place. Tamp the concrete around the posts with a piece of wood.

5 Building other frames
Follow the same procedures for all the walkway frames, all the while using the spirit level to ensure that the frames are level with each other. Build the raised decking corner units in the same way, concreting the 24-in.-long posts into holes 12-in. deep.

6 Fastening the decking
Screw the decking boards across the joists with 3-in.-long screws. To complete the engawa, sand down the whole structure. Mix the white paint with a good quantity of water to make a thin wash, and give the engawa two coats. See page 58 for building the steps.

Circular patio

The circular patio is intriguing to look at—reminiscent of a waterwheel, or maybe part of a windmill. Its arresting appearance makes the perfect setting for a water feature or a flower display, and the rugged decking provides a good, level surface for all types of other backyard activities. You can easily save on material costs by using salvaged wood, such as old floorboards, if necessary.

Easy

Making time
One weekend
One day for building the hexagonal frames; one day for putting it together and finishing

Considering the design

The patio is constructed from wedge-shaped segments cut from 18 pine planks, measuring 40 inches long, 10 inches wide and 1 inch thick. This quantity provides 35 wedges and allows a spare one left over for good measure. The diameter of the patio is about 8 feet.

We set the patio in an existing circle of gravel. If you want to create a similar gravel area specifically for your patio, you will need about eight wheelbarrow loads of fine gravel. The wedge-shaped decking boards are fastened to three hexagonal frames. When the whole patio

construction is in place, the frames are held secure by the gravel, and the boards are supported and displayed to their best advantage.

Getting started

Inspect your site and decide where you want the patio to be placed. Use pegs and string to lay out a circular area somewhat over 8 feet in diameter, and cover it with gravel. Edge the circle with a material of your choice. We have used edging shaped like split logs from a garden center, and we arranged a few cobblestones in the space between the patio and the edging.

You will need

Tools

- Pencil, ruler, tape measure, and square
- Pegs and string
- Two portable workbenches
- Miter saw
- Rip saw
- Cordless power drill with a cross-head screwdriver bit
- Drill bits to match the sizes of the screws
- Rake

Materials

(All rough-sawn pieces of pine include excess length for wastage. All the wood is pressure-treated with preservative.)

For a patio 8 ft. in diameter

- Pine: 9 rough-sawn 1 x 10s, 7 ft. long (wedge boards)
- Pine: 8 rough-sawn 1 x 3s, 6 ft. 6 in. long, (hexagonal frames)
- Zinc-plated, countersunk cross-head screws: 50 x 3-in.-long no. 10, 200 x 2-in.-long no. 8

Overall dimensions and general notes

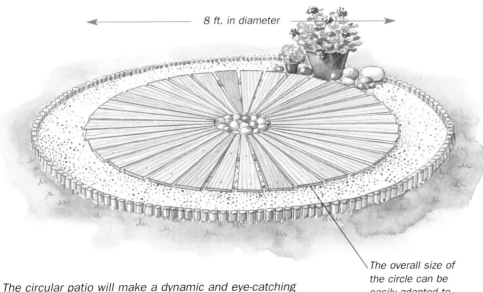

8 ft. in diameter

The circular patio will make a dynamic and eye-catching feature, whether in a small town plot or a larger garden.

The overall size of the circle can be easily adapted to suit any garden

Exploded view of the circular patio

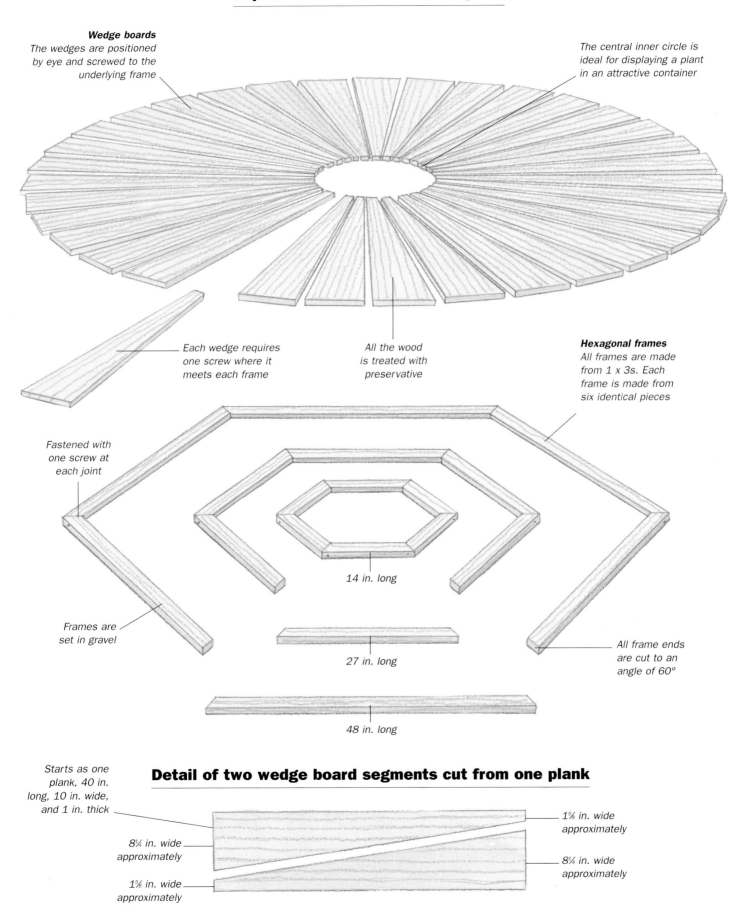

Wedge boards
The wedges are positioned by eye and screwed to the underlying frame

The central inner circle is ideal for displaying a plant in an attractive container

Each wedge requires one screw where it meets each frame

All the wood is treated with preservative

Hexagonal frames
All frames are made from 1 x 3s. Each frame is made from six identical pieces

Fastened with one screw at each joint

Frames are set in gravel

14 in. long

27 in. long

All frame ends are cut to an angle of 60°

48 in. long

Starts as one plank, 40 in. long, 10 in. wide, and 1 in. thick

Detail of two wedge board segments cut from one plank

8¼ in. wide approximately

1⅝ in. wide approximately

1⅝ in. wide approximately

8¼ in. wide approximately

Making the circular patio

1 Cutting the wedges
Cut the wedge boards into 40-in. lengths, and mark them off into two parts, as shown on page 40. Use the rip saw to cut them diagonally along their length, so that you have two wedges.

2 Cutting the frames
Mark out the pieces that make the three hexagonal frames. Set the miter saw to make a 60°/30° cut and saw the wood to length. You need six identical lengths for each hexagon.

3 Fastening the frames
Lay out the pieces for each of the three frames and fasten them together with 3-in.-long screws. Drill pilot holes before driving in the screws so that you do not split the wood.

4 Positioning the frames
Position the three frames, one within another, on the gravel circle. Stand back and look at them from several angles to ensure that they are centered and correctly aligned, then rake the gravel level with the top of the frames.

5 Fastening the wedges
Set all the wedge-shaped boards in place. Check by eye and make adjustments until you are happy with the arrangement, then fasaten them with 2-in.-long screws, using one screw for each board–frame intersection.

Country walkway

This sweeping walkway looks good in both rural and urban settings, and it will remain dry, firm, and level despite assault by the weather and wear and tear by humans. It is simplicity itself—there is no need to mix concrete for securing posts or to lay plastic sheet to stop the growth of weeds. If you like the notion of a low-key walkway, and you want to build it quickly and easily, this is a good project to try.

★
Easy

Making time
One weekend for a 20 ft. walkway
One day for trenches and cutting wood; one day for construction

Considering the design

The walkway measures approximately 3 feet wide. It is made from two types of posts—20-inch lengths of turned, round-section wood (6 inches in diameter) for the edging, and 20-inch lengths of 4 x 4s for the walkway blocks. Once the edging is in place, the walkway blocks are carefully positioned about 2 inches apart on a base of large-size gravel or shingle, then the spaces in and around the blocks are filled in with a layer of fine gravel. The blocks are firm and level, making a good, safe walkway, which is perfect for all users of the garden and their activities, whether it is strolling, pushing a wheelbarrow, or playing.

Getting started

Use the tape measure, pegs, and string to lay out the route of the walkway. Note that you need six round-section posts (3 feet long), and three square-section posts (3 feet long) for each yard in length of walkway (all posts will be cut in half). Clear the route of plants, and dig out the area to a depth of 8 inches. Establish the position of the two trenches.

Overall dimensions and general notes

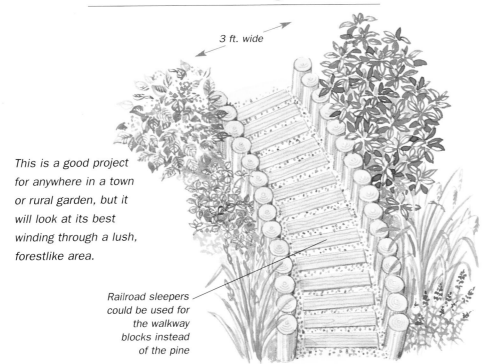

3 ft. wide

This is a good project for anywhere in a town or rural garden, but it will look at its best winding through a lush, forestlike area.

Railroad sleepers could be used for the walkway blocks instead of the pine

Exploded view of the country walkway

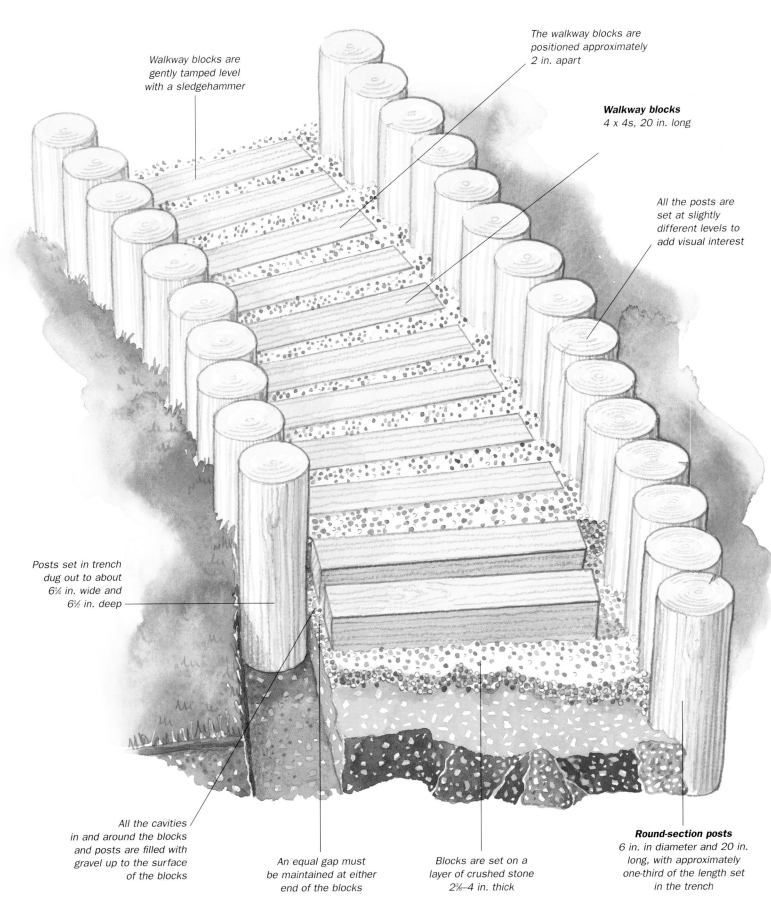

Walkway blocks are gently tamped level with a sledgehammer

The walkway blocks are positioned approximately 2 in. apart

Walkway blocks
4 x 4s, 20 in. long

All the posts are set at slightly different levels to add visual interest

Posts set in trench dug out to about 6¼ in. wide and 6½ in. deep

All the cavities in and around the blocks and posts are filled with gravel up to the surface of the blocks

An equal gap must be maintained at either end of the blocks

Blocks are set on a layer of crushed stone 2⅜–4 in. thick

Round-section posts
6 in. in diameter and 20 in. long, with approximately one-third of the length set in the trench

Making the country walkway

1 Laying out the walkway
Use the tape measure, pegs, and string to lay out the route of the walkway. Dig out the area to 8 in. deep and a total of 3 ft.wide. Dig a trench along one side of the walkway 6¼ in. wide and 6½ in. deep, and set in a row of 20-in.-long round-section posts.

2 Completing the posts
Repeat the procedure for the other side of the walkway. Use the excavated soil to fill around the posts and to generally level the area. Tamp with the sledgehammer.

3 Spreading crushed stone
Shovel a layer of crushed stone or gravel over the ground between the posts, then spread and level it with the rake, making it 2⅜–4 in. thick. Tamp the crushed stone into the soil until it is firm underfoot.

4 Laying the walkway blocks
Take the 20-in.-long 4 x 4s for the walkway blocks, and place them on the crushed stone, about 2 in. apart and centered within the width of the walkway. Adjust them so that they radiate around the curves. Lay the gravel.

Japanese bridge

★★
Intermediate

The Japanese bridge allows you to cross over a narrow expanse of water. It is made by spanning the water with two beams 4 inches in diameter, which are covered with 2 x 4 decking. There is a handrail to one side of the bridge made from bamboo. The handrail posts are bolted directly to the side of one beam and braced and triangulated to the underside of the other.

Making time
One weekend
One day for the main beams and decking, and one day for the bamboo handrail

Considering the design

The bridge is 12 feet long—if you want, you can make it shorter, but for reasons of safety it cannot be made any longer. The handrail is fastened to the posts with mortise-and-tenon joints, pegs are driven into the sides of the posts, and the joints are lashed together with cord.

Getting started

Clear the foliage from the bank sides and check that the ground is firm. Inspect the main beams to make sure that they are free from splits and deep knots.

Overall dimensions and general notes

24 in. wide

12 ft. long

We have chosen to build this bridge over a pond, but it would also look good built over a dry "river" of gravel in the Japanese tradition.

You will need

Tools

- ✓ Pencil, ruler, tape measure, and square
- ✓ Pegs and string
- ✓ Two portable workbenches
- ✓ Crosscut saw
- ✓ Spade and sledgehammer
- ✓ Claw hammer
- ✓ Ax
- ✓ Wrench to fasten the bolts
- ✓ Cordless power drill with a cross-head screwdriver bit, 1-in. flat bit
- ✓ Drill bits to match the sizes of the screws, nails, and bolts
- ✓ Saber saw
- ✓ Sander

Materials

(All rough-sawn pieces of pine include excess length for wastage. All the wood is pressure-treated with preservative. Nails are purchased to the nearest lb. measure.)

For a bridge 12 ft. long and 24 in. wide

- ✓ Pine: 2 round-section pieces, 4 in. in diameter, 13 ft. long (main beams)
- ✓ Pine: 2 round-section pieces, 4 in. in diameter, 10 ft. long (support piles, handrail posts, and rail pegs)
- ✓ Pine: 15 rough-sawn 2 x 4s, 6 ft. 6 in. long (decking and bracing)
- ✓ Pine: 1 rough-sawn 1 x 2, 13 ft. long, (temporary guide)
- ✓ Bamboo: 1 piece, 4 in. in diameter, 10 ft. long (handrail)

- ✓ Bamboo: 2 pieces, 10 ft. long (secondary rails)
- ✓ Cord: 65 ft. of heavy-duty natural fiber cord (for binding the joints)
- ✓ Nails: 2 lb. of 6-in.-long (60 d) nails (for fastening the main beams to the piles)
- ✓ Nails: 5 lbs. of 5-in.-long (40 d) nails (for fastening the decking to the beams)
- ✓ Zinc-plated, countersunk cross-head screws: 50 x 3½ in.-long no. 10
- ✓ Carriage bolts: 2 x 10 in. long, with nuts and washers to fit

Exploded view of the Japanese bridge

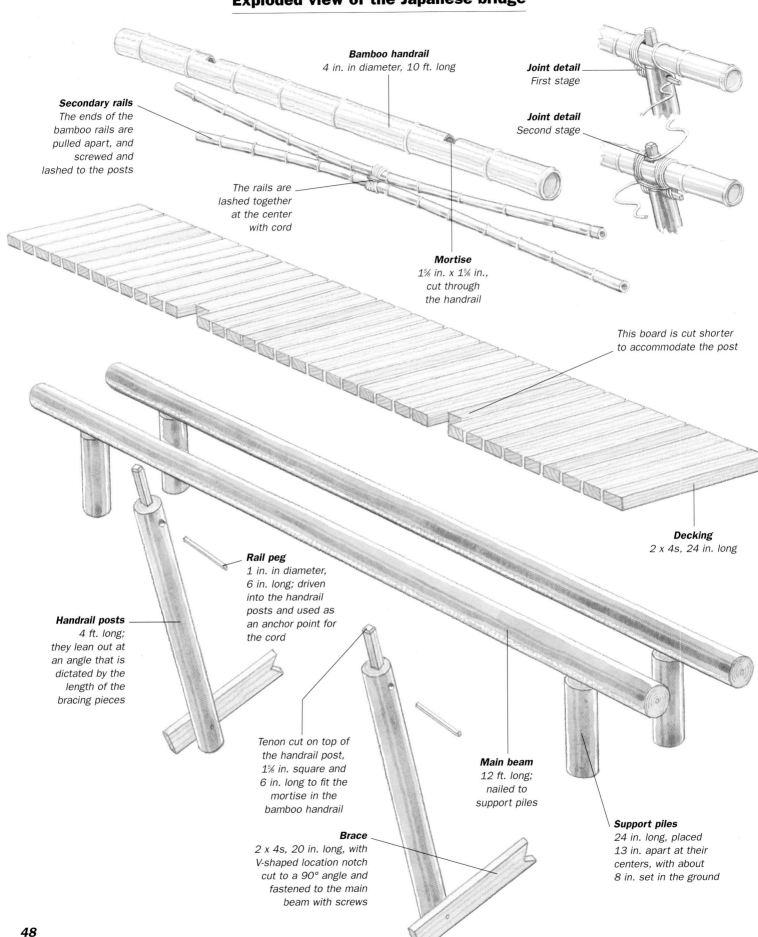

Bamboo handrail
4 in. in diameter, 10 ft. long

Joint detail
First stage

Joint detail
Second stage

Secondary rails
The ends of the bamboo rails are pulled apart, and screwed and lashed to the posts

The rails are lashed together at the center with cord

Mortise
1⅝ in. x 1⅝ in., cut through the handrail

This board is cut shorter to accommodate the post

Decking
2 x 4s, 24 in. long

Rail peg
1 in. in diameter, 6 in. long; driven into the handrail posts and used as an anchor point for the cord

Handrail posts
4 ft. long; they lean out at an angle that is dictated by the length of the bracing pieces

Tenon cut on top of the handrail post, 1⅝ in. square and 6 in. long to fit the mortise in the bamboo handrail

Main beam
12 ft. long; nailed to support piles

Support piles
24 in. long, placed 13 in. apart at their centers, with about 8 in. set in the ground

Brace
2 x 4s, 20 in. long, with V-shaped location notch cut to a 90° angle and fastened to the main beam with screws

Making the Japanese bridge

1 Fastening the main beams
Cut four 24-in.-long support piles and dig them in at either side of the water, so that they are level and 13 in. apart at their centers, and 16 in. above ground level. Nail the main beams directly to the top of the posts, using 6-in. long nails.

2 Fastening the decking
Center and nail one 24-in.-long decking board at either end of the main beams. Nail the temporary 1 x 2 guide to the ends of the boards, then nail all the decking boards in place. Leave two gaps for the handrail posts. Use 5-in.-long nails throughout.

3 Making the handrail
Cut the handrail posts to length. Use the saw and ax to cut tenons $1\frac{5}{8}$ in. square and 6 in. long on what will be the top end of each post. Use carriage bolts to bolt the handrail posts securely to the main beams (see illustration, step 4).

4 Bracing
Cut the two braces to length. Cut a right-angled V-shaped location notch on one end of each brace. Use screws to fasten the braces between the end of the posts and the underside of the beams.

5 Fastening the handrail
Mark in the position of the mortise holes on the bamboo handrail, and cut them out with the drill and saber saw. Sit the handrail on the tenons. Drill holes, bang in the rail pegs, and lash the joints with the cord.

6 Adding secondary rails
Lash the two bamboo secondary rails together at the center, and drill and drive them to the posts with screws. Finally, bind over the screws with the cord. Sand everything to a good finish.

Planter containers

Planter containers make a great addition to any outdoor space. They can be filled with an ever-changing display to inject color into the yard throughout the year. Wood has an instant appeal when combined with plants—as a natural material, it instantly harmonizes. These planters are built with a variety of cut and curved pickets, in folksy style, or with square pickets topped with a mitered frame, for a clean, modern look.

★ ★
Intermediate

Making time
One weekend
One day for building the frames and cutting the pickets, and one day for putting together

Considering the design

Each of the three planters is built from two horizontal frames, with pickets fastened vertically to the outside so that the frames are hidden from view.

We have made a large planter with square pickets, trimmed on top with a decorative mitered frame, a medium planter with rounded pickets, and a small planter with pointed pickets. If you follow our suggestions exactly, this variety of styles will provide an eclectic look for your patio. Alternatively, you can opt for a more traditional look and make a set of three planters to the same design.

The frames are built from lengths of 1 x 2s, the pickets are cut from 1 x 3s, and the right-angled corner fillet pieces are cut from 2 x 3s. The wood will be sanded smooth after the planter is constructed.

Getting started

If you want to vary the design, shape, size, and quantity of the planters, sit down with a pencil and paper and work out the materials, then order the wood accordingly. For each planter, you will have to decide on the design of the top, the total height, and the length and width of the sides.

You will need

Tools

- ✔ Pencil, ruler, compass, tape measure, bevel gauge, and square
- ✔ Two portable workbenches
- ✔ Crosscut saw
- ✔ Power drill with a cross-head screwdriver bit
- ✔ Drill bits to match the sizes of the screws
- ✔ Claw hammer
- ✔ Saber saw and sander

Materials

(All rough-sawn pieces of pine include excess length for wastage. All the wood is pressure-treated with preservative. Make sure this is of a type that is not harmful to plants.)

For a large, medium, and small planter container

- ✔ Pine: 5 rough-sawn 1 x 2s, 10 ft. long, (frames)
- ✔ Pine: 1 rough-sawn 2 x 3, 6 ft. 6 in. long (corner fillets)
- ✔ Pine: 15 rough-sawn 1 x 3s, 10 ft. long, (pickets, decorative mitered frame, floorboards)
- ✔ Zinc-plated, countersunk cross-head screws: 200 x 1⅛-in.-long no. 8, 200 x 2-inch-long no. 8
- ✔ Galvanized nails: 5 lb. of 1¾-inch-long (5 d) nails

Overall dimensions and general notes

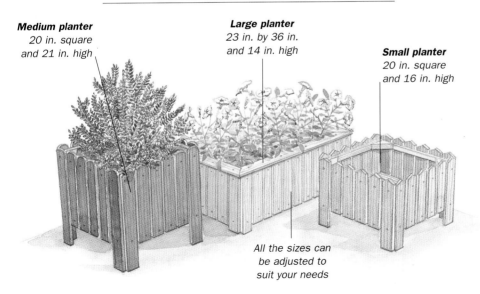

Medium planter
20 in. square
and 21 in. high

Large planter
23 in. by 36 in.
and 14 in. high

Small planter
20 in. square
and 16 in. high

All the sizes can be adjusted to suit your needs

Planter containers can brighten up an area of decking, a patio, or a balcony. They can be filled directly with soil; alternatively, plants in containers can be arranged inside them.

Exploded view of the large planter container

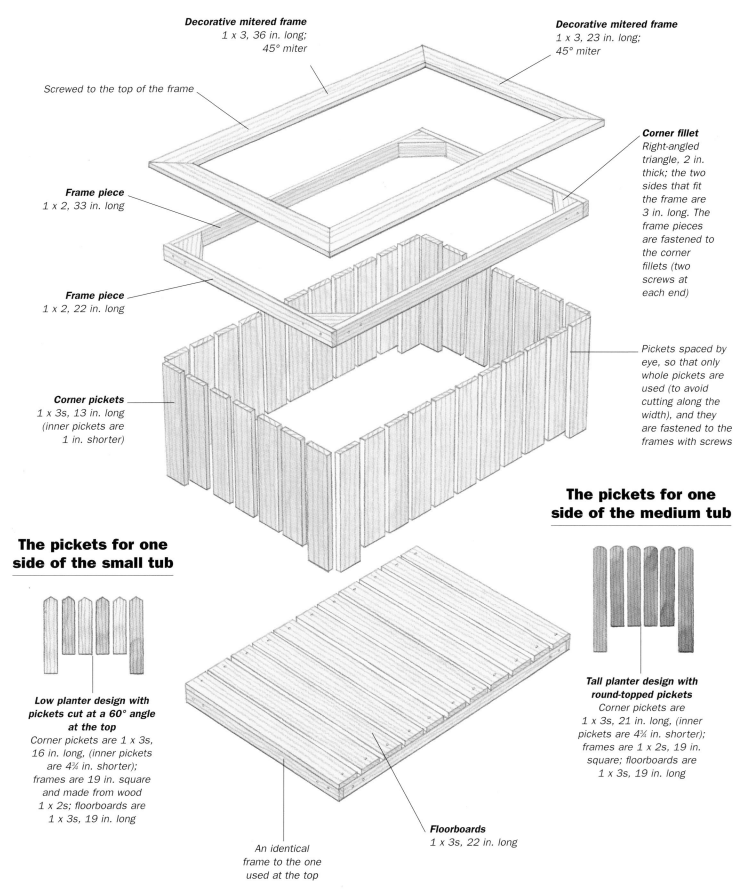

Decorative mitered frame
1 x 3, 36 in. long;
45° miter

Decorative mitered frame
1 x 3, 23 in. long;
45° miter

Screwed to the top of the frame

Corner fillet
Right-angled triangle, 2 in. thick; the two sides that fit the frame are 3 in. long. The frame pieces are fastened to the corner fillets (two screws at each end)

Frame piece
1 x 2, 33 in. long

Frame piece
1 x 2, 22 in. long

Pickets spaced by eye, so that only whole pickets are used (to avoid cutting along the width), and they are fastened to the frames with screws

Corner pickets
1 x 3s, 13 in. long (inner pickets are 1 in. shorter)

The pickets for one side of the medium tub

The pickets for one side of the small tub

Low planter design with pickets cut at a 60° angle at the top
Corner pickets are 1 x 3s, 16 in. long, (inner pickets are 4¾ in. shorter); frames are 19 in. square and made from wood 1 x 2s; floorboards are 1 x 3s, 19 in. long

Tall planter design with round-topped pickets
Corner pickets are 1 x 3s, 21 in. long, (inner pickets are 4¾ in. shorter); frames are 1 x 2s, 19 in. square; floorboards are 1 x 3s, 19 in. long

An identical frame to the one used at the top

Floorboards
1 x 3s, 22 in. long

Making the planter containers

1 Constructing the frames
Cut the component parts for the frames, and the corner fillets, to length. Set the parts together, drill pilot holes, and fasten them with 2-in.-long screws. Make two frames for each container.

2 Fastening the corner pickets
Cut the corner pickets to length, and fasten them to the corners of the top frame with 1⅛-in.-long screws. Note how the extended length of the corner pickets creates the leg feature.

3 Making the floor
Cut the floorboards to length and nail them to the bottom frame. Drill pilot holes for the nails to avoid splitting the wood. Space the floorboards by eye so that you use only whole boards to cover the frame (this avoids having to cut down the length of a board).

4 Putting together
Using 1⅝-in.-long screws, fasten the bottom frame to the corner pickets. Check that the structure is square, and screw all the inner pickets in place on both frames. Space the pickets by eye so that you use only whole ones to cover each side of the planter.

5 Decorative frame
The large planter has a decorative mitered frame on the top. Cut pieces of wood to fit both the length and width of the planter. Miter the corners with the saber saw, and screw the frame to the top of the planter with 1⅝-in.-long screws to cover the tops of the pickets.

6 Shaped pickets
If you are going to use shaped pickets (curved for the medium planter and pointed for the small planter), draw curves or mark center points on the pickets with the compass. Use the saber saw to cut out the profile. Finally, sand all the planters to a smooth finish.

Checkerboard decking patio

★ ★
Intermediate

Making time
One weekend
One day for building the gridded frame, and the rest of the time for fitting the decking

The good thing about the checkerboard patio is its flexibility. The design allows it to be square, rectangular, castellated, or just about any shape that inspires you, as long as the sum total shape can be made up from a square grid. The checkerboard grid construction also permits you to keep selected squares free in order to plant flowers, or site a bench seat, sandpit, water feature, tree, or area of grass.

Considering the design

The frame is set face down on a bed of gravel. It is made up of eight joists spaced 14 inches apart in one direction, topped by a second layer set at right angles in the other direction. The resulting grid is secured and held square by fastening 12-inch-long filler pieces to the bottom layer. Finally, the decking boards are simply attached to the gridded frame.

The techniques are straightforward—there are no difficult-to-use tools involved or complex jointing to do—but this very simplicity calls for extra care and effort at the designing and planning stage in order to get good results.

Getting started

Inspect your site and decide whether you want the patio to follow the dimensions of the project (8 ft. 6 in. square). Use a tape measure, pegs, and string to mark it out. Transfer the shape to grid paper, so that the joists are 14 inches apart at their centers. Work out how much wood is needed if dimensions have altered.

You will need

Tools

✔ Pencil, ruler, tape measure, square, bevel gauge, grid paper

✔ Pegs and string

✔ Spade and wheelbarrow

✔ Power drill with a cross-head screwdriver bit

✔ Drill bits to match the sizes of the screws

✔ Crosscut saw

✔ Two portable workbenches

✔ Sander

✔ Paintbrush

Materials

(All rough-sawn pieces of pine include excess length for wastage. All the wood is pressure-treated with preservative.)

For a patio 8 ft. 6 in. square

✔ Pine: 24 rough-sawn 1 x 3s, 10 ft. long, (frame and filler pieces)

✔ Pine: 33 rough-sawn 1 x 4s, 10 ft. long, (decking boards)

✔ Zinc-plated, countersunk cross-head screws: 100 x 2¼-in.-long no. 8, 200 x 1⅜-in-long no. 8

✔ Plastic ground sheeting: 10 ft. by 10 ft.

✔ Gravel: 10 wheelbarrow loads

✔ Exterior-grade decking paint

Overall dimensions and general notes

8 ft. 6 in.

Selected squares are left uncovered in order to incorporate plants and cobblestones

This is an excellent project where space is limited. The patio can also be used to reduce the monotony of a large area of lawn. It could even be painted in bold colors.

Exploded view of the checkerboard decking patio

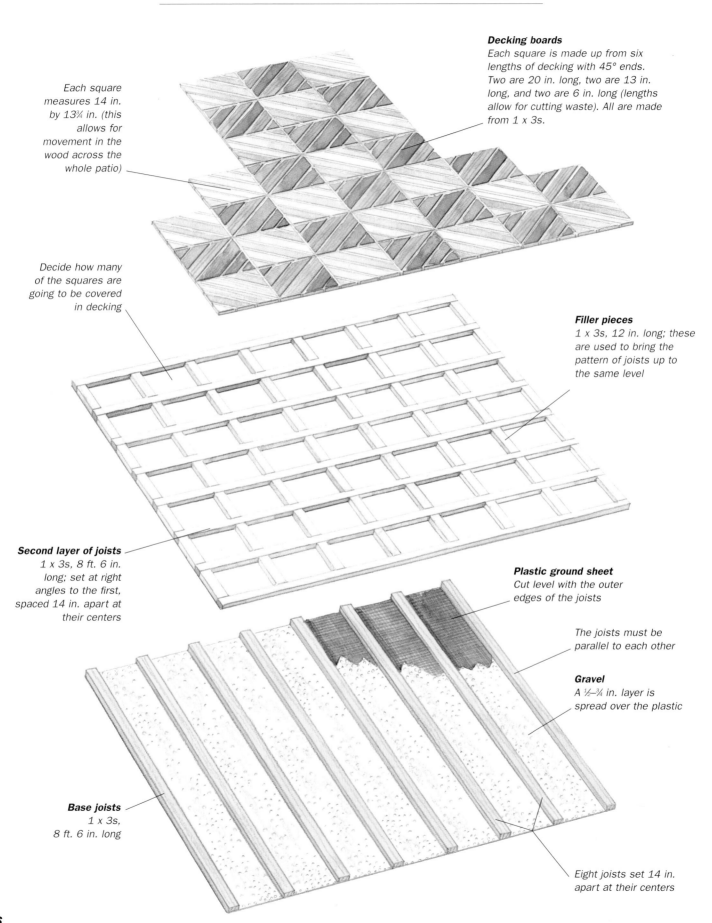

Decking boards
Each square is made up from six lengths of decking with 45° ends. Two are 20 in. long, two are 13 in. long, and two are 6 in. long (lengths allow for cutting waste). All are made from 1 x 3s.

Each square measures 14 in. by 13¾ in. (this allows for movement in the wood across the whole patio)

Decide how many of the squares are going to be covered in decking

Filler pieces
1 x 3s, 12 in. long; these are used to bring the pattern of joists up to the same level

Second layer of joists
1 x 3s, 8 ft. 6 in. long; set at right angles to the first, spaced 14 in. apart at their centers

Plastic ground sheet
Cut level with the outer edges of the joists

The joists must be parallel to each other

Gravel
A ½–¾ in. layer is spread over the plastic

Base joists
1 x 3s, 8 ft. 6 in. long

Eight joists set 14 in. apart at their centers

Making the checkerboard decking patio

1 Placing the base joists

Spread the plastic sheeting over the site and cover it with a ½–¾ in. layer of washed gravel. Take eight joists and position them side by side, so that they are parallel to each other and set 14 in. apart at the centers.

2 Placing the second layer

Take eight more joists and position them on top of the base joists in the manner just described, so they are side by side in a grid pattern and set 14 in. apart at the centers. Drive 2¼-in.-long screws down through the intersections to fasten the layers together.

3 Adding filler pieces

Cut 12-in. lengths of the 1 x 3s to make filler pieces for the grid. Place these over the visible parts of the first layer of joists to bring them up to the level of the second layer. Screw the filler pieces in place with 2¼-in.-long screws.

4 Cutting the decking

Look at the grid frame, decide on the edge profile and where you want any planting holes to occur, and calculate how many squares you need to cover with decking. Cut and miter six lengths of decking board (see page 56 for measurements) for each square.

5 Fitting the decking

Set the decking boards on the frame in the pattern and configuration that you have planned, and fasten them in place with 1⅜-in.-long screws. Sand the structure. Finally, thin the paint with water, and brush it on to create a thin coat of color.

Decking area with steps

Decking is great for a sloping site. You don't have the task of moving vast quantities of soil to create a level area, because you simply float the decking over the problem by adjusting the length of the legs to accommodate the slope of the ground. Once the decking is in place, you will suddenly be able to see the garden in a whole new light— the experience is somewhat like sitting on a flying carpet.

Intermediate

Making time
Two weekends
One day for casting the foot piers, two days for building the decking, one day for finishing

Considering the design

This large, square platform has a post at each corner, and a small flight of steps centered on one side. The platform frame is bolted directly to the legs, which are socketed into concrete piers.

Getting started

Measure out the site, clear the ground, and establish where the concrete piers will go. Decide where you want to attach the steps. Arrange the wood in ordered stacks, and recruit friends for future help at the leveling stage, when you will have to bolt the frame to the legs.

Overall dimensions and general notes

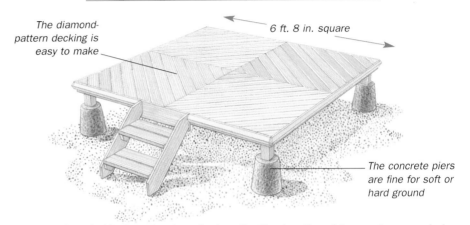

The diamond-pattern decking is easy to make

6 ft. 8 in. square

The concrete piers are fine for soft or hard ground

This decking is suitable for a level or sloping site (the lengths of the posts are varied accordingly) and is ideal for sunbathing or as the site for a table and a couple of chairs.

You will need

Tools

- ✔ Pencil, ruler, tape measure, marking gauge, and square
- ✔ Two portable workbenches
- ✔ Crosscut saw, spade, shovel
- ✔ Wheelbarrow, bucket, spirit level
- ✔ Power drill with a cross-head screwdriver bit
- ✔ Drill bits to match the sizes of the nails, screws, and bolts
- ✔ Claw hammer, ratchet wrench
- ✔ Sander

Materials

(All pieces of rough-sawn wood include excess length for wastage. All the wood is pressure-treated with preservative.)

For decking 6 ft. 8 in. square and about 20 in. high

- ✔ Pine: 1 rough-sawn 3 x 3, 6 ft. 6 in. long, (leg posts, support blocks, and molding blocks)
- ✔ Pine: 10 rough-sawn 2 x 3s, 6 ft. 6 in. long, (frame and joists)
- ✔ Pine: 25 pieces of 1-x-4 planed and grooved decking boards, 6 ft. 6 in. long (floor)
- ✔ Pine: 4 pieces of rough-sawn, pitch-top 1 x 3 fence capping, 6 ft. 6 in. long, (frame trim)
- ✔ Pine: 1 rough-sawn 1 x 6, 10 ft. long (stringers)
- ✔ Pine: grooved 2 x 5 decking, 10 ft. long (treads)
- ✔ Pine: 1 rough-sawn 1 x 3, 3 ft. long, (brackets)
- ✔ Zinc-plated carriage bolts, washers, and nuts: 8 x 6-in.-long bolts
- ✔ Zinc-plated, countersunk cross-head screws: 300 x 4-in.-long no. 8, 300 x 3-in.-long no. 10, 50 x 2-in.-long no. 8
- ✔ Steel nails: 2 lbs., 5 in. long (40 d)
- ✔ Concrete: 1 part (55 lb.) Portland cement, 2 parts (110 lb.) sand, 3 parts (165 lb.) aggregate
- ✔ Six plastic flowerpots: about 10 in. high, 9 in. wide at the rim, and 7 in. wide at the base
- ✔ Adhesive tape

Exploded view of the decking area with steps

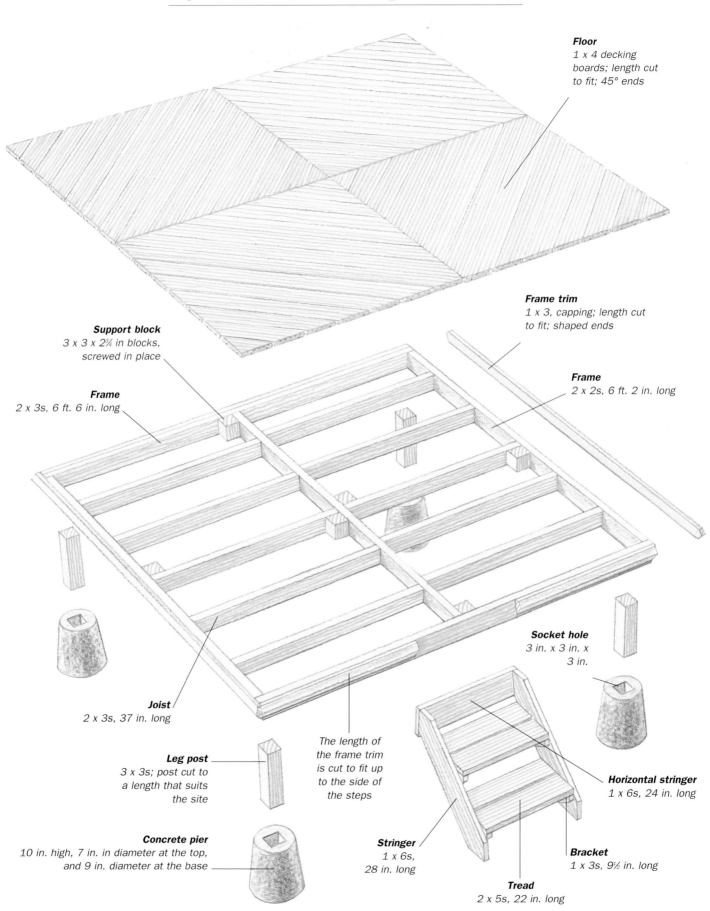

Floor
1 x 4 decking boards; length cut to fit; 45° ends

Frame trim
1 x 3, capping; length cut to fit; shaped ends

Frame
2 x 2s, 6 ft. 2 in. long

Support block
3 x 3 x 2¾ in blocks, screwed in place

Frame
2 x 3s, 6 ft. 6 in. long

Socket hole
3 in. x 3 in. x 3 in.

Joist
2 x 3s, 37 in. long

Leg post
3 x 3s; post cut to a length that suits the site

The length of the frame trim is cut to fit up to the side of the steps

Horizontal stringer
1 x 6s, 24 in. long

Concrete pier
10 in. high, 7 in. in diameter at the top, and 9 in. diameter at the base

Stringer
1 x 6s, 28 in. long

Bracket
1 x 3s, 9½ in. long

Tread
2 x 5s, 22 in. long

Making the decking area with steps

1 Making the concrete pers
Cut six 3-in.-long molding blocks from the 3-in.-square wood and set one in the bottom of each plastic flowerpot. Cover the hole at the bottom with adhesive tape and fill the pots with concrete. (Two extra pots have been allowed in case of mistakes.)

2 Making the frame
Cut the wood for the frame (see page 60). Build a frame 6 ft. 6 in. square, with a central joist crossing between opposite sides. Fasten 3 x 3 support blocks (see diagram) to strengthen the primary T-junction joints. Use 4-in.-long screws throughout.

3 Fastening the secondary joists
Set the secondary joists in place in each quarter of the frame—so that they form a tight wedge fit—and secure them in place with nails. Ease the concrete foot piers out of the flowerpots and remove the wood to reveal the sockets.

4 Setting the frame on its legs
With friends to help, cut one post for each leg, and push them into the sockets in the concrete piers. Bolt the legs inside the corners of the frame, and check that the frame is level. Saw the top of the leg posts level with the top edge of the frame.

5 Making the steps
Construct the steps from the treads, stringers, and brackets, and fasten them to the frame, using 3-in.-long screws. Cut the frame trim to fit, shaping the ends to create neat corners to cover the sawn ends of the decking. Secure it to the frame with 2-in.-long screws.

6 Making the floor
Cut the decking boards for the floor to size, and screw them to the top surface of the joists with 3-in.-long screws. Finally, use the sander to smooth all the sawn ends to a slightly rounded, splinter-free finish.

Bench seat and safety rail

★★
Intermediate

Making time
Two weekends
*Two days for the
bench seat and two
days for the rail*

If you would like to have a bench seat to put on an area of decking, try this project. Because it is potentially dangerous if a bench is placed near the edge of the decking, we have designed a rail to act as a safety barrier. The rail and baluster design can easily be modified to match the style of existing decking. If you want, the bench can be bolted to both the decking and the rail to make an extra-strong structure.

Considering the design

Both items have been designed so that they can be made from off-the-shelf sections. In many of our projects, function follows form, meaning that the way the design looks in the garden is as least as important as the way the project functions, so that it doesn't matter too much if you make changes to the design.

However, in this instance, function is all-important, and both the bench and rail must be safe before any other considerations. (This is especially true for rails. They must be exactly the right height, and fastened so that they can stand a fair amount of wear and tear.) So you must

think very carefully before you make any major structural changes to the designs.

Finally, we used exterior-grade paint to add an attractive finish to the design.

Getting started

Examine your decking and consider the best site for the bench and rail. The weight of the bench must be equally distributed over the joists of the decking, and the rail must be bolted to one or more of the primary joists. We have fastened rails to two sides of a relatively low decking patio, but if you have an area of decking that is raised high off the ground, it is best to fit rails on all sides.

You will need

Tools

✔ Pencil, ruler, tape measure, square
✔ Two portable workbenches
✔ Crosscut saw
✔ Power drill with a cross-head screwdriver bit
✔ Drill bits to match the sizes of the screws and bolts
✔ Ratchet wrench and spirit level
✔ Sander

Materials

(All rough-sawn pine includes excess length for wastage. All wood is pressure-treated with preservative.)

For a bench with sides 5 ft. 4 in. long; rails 7 ft. long, 37 in.high

✔ Pine: 3 rough-sawn 3 x 3s, 6 ft. 6 in. long (posts and bench legs)
✔ Pine: 26 rough-sawn 1 x 2s, 6 ft. 6 in. long (balusters and baluster rails)
✔ Pine: 7 rough-sawn 1 x 4s, 10 ft. long (rails, seat boards, fascia)
✔ Pine: 1 rough-sawn 2 x 4, 10 ft. long (under-seat stretcher)
✔ Zinc-plated, countersunk cross-head screws: 50 x 3½-in.-long no. 10, 100 x 1⅜-in.-long no. 8
✔ Carriage bolts: 12 x 6-in.-long, with nuts and washers to fit

Overall dimensions and general notes

7 ft. long

The boards on the top of the bench form a herringbone design where they meet in the corner

37 in. high

5 ft. 4 in. long

This bench-and-safety-rail combination is suitable for adding to a wide range of decking patios, and it is simple to build. It makes a safe place for all the family to relax.

Exploded view of the bench seat and safety rail

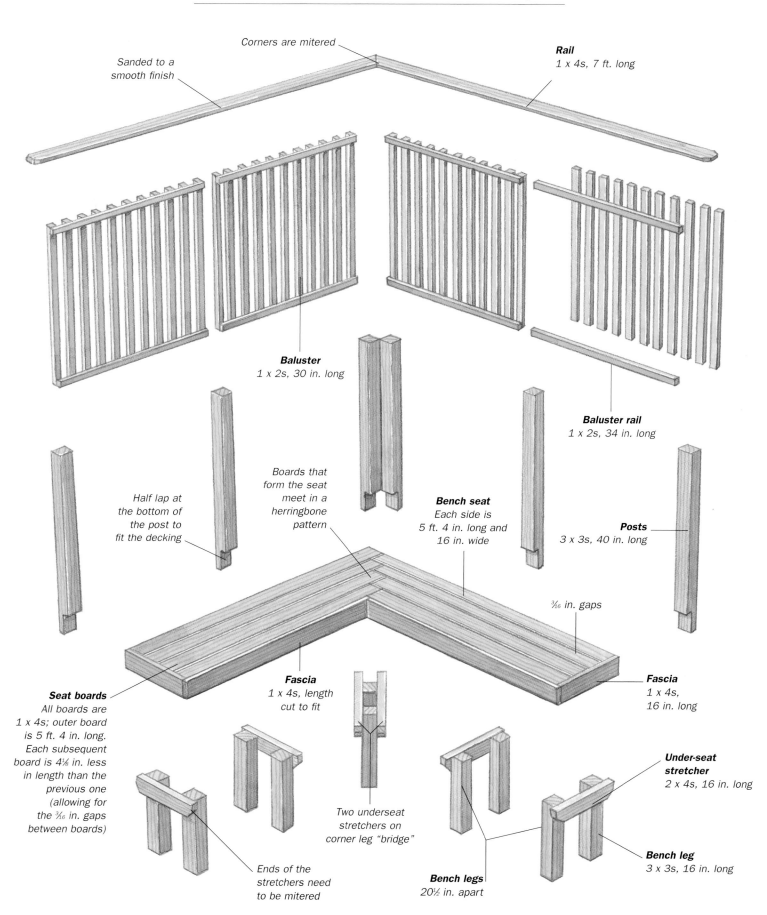

Corners are mitered

Sanded to a smooth finish

Rail
1 x 4s, 7 ft. long

Baluster
1 x 2s, 30 in. long

Baluster rail
1 x 2s, 34 in. long

Half lap at the bottom of the post to fit the decking

Boards that form the seat meet in a herringbone pattern

Bench seat
Each side is 5 ft. 4 in. long and 16 in. wide

Posts
3 x 3s, 40 in. long

³⁄₁₆ in. gaps

Seat boards
All boards are 1 x 4s; outer board is 5 ft. 4 in. long. Each subsequent board is 4⅛ in. less in length than the previous one (allowing for the ³⁄₁₆ in. gaps between boards)

Fascia
1 x 4s, length cut to fit

Fascia
1 x 4s, 16 in. long

Under-seat stretcher
2 x 4s, 16 in. long

Two underseat stretchers on corner leg "bridge"

Ends of the stretchers need to be mitered

Bench legs
20½ in. apart

Bench leg
3 x 3s, 16 in. long

Making the bench seat and safety rail

1 Cutting the posts
Cut the six posts for the uprights of the safety rail assembly to length, cutting half lap joints on one end to fit the ring joist (outer frame) of the existing decking. Set the posts in place.

2 Fastening the posts and rails
Fasten the posts to the decking joists with 3½-in.-long screws and the carriage bolts. Use the spirit level to ensure that the posts are upright. Cut the two rails to length, with a 45° miter at the corner, and screw them to the top of the posts with 3½-in.-long screws.

3 Building the balusters
For the baluster rails and balusters, build four frames. Set them in place between the posts, and screw them in position. Drive screws down through the rails and into the top of the baluster frames. Use 3½-in.-long screws throughout.

4 Making the bench legs
Build the five "bridge" frames that make the legs of the bench—the four frames for the straight sides, and the double-top frame for the corner of the bench. Use 3½-in.-long screws throughout to fasten the pieces.

5 Fastening bench legs and seat
Set the leg "bridge" frames in place on the decking and link them with the seat boards, using 1⅜-in.-long screws. Note the way the boards are cut and fastened in a herringbone pattern at the corner.

6 Making a fascia
Cover the front edges and ends of the bench with a fascia that runs flush to the surface of the bench. Use 1⅜-in.-long screws throughout. Finally, sand everything to a smooth finish.

Tree ring seat

When I was a child I used to love sitting on an old ring seat under an apple tree in my grandparents' orchard. I can picture the scene now—the trunk of the old tree to my back, a dappled canopy of leaves overhead, and long, lush grass underfoot. If you have a suitable small tree, this seat will come into its own in summer when you can use it to relax under the leafy shade. Remember to allow room for the trunk to grow.

Making time
One weekend
One day for making the parts and one day for assembling the seat around the tree

Considering the design

The seat is based on a hexagon and built in easy-to-make sections. The idea is that the sections can be prepared in a convenient location—perhaps in the workshop or the garage—then put together around your chosen tree.

The seat stands 16¾ inches above ground level. The legs are built from 2-inch-wide sections, and each pair of legs is bridged with top stretchers. These leg units are joined to each other with linking stretchers, making the hexagonal design seen in plan view. The construction is topped with a seat made from 4-inch-wide decking boards (we have used grooved decking), and the front edge is trimmed with a decorative wavy frieze, or apron.

Getting started

Select an appropriate tree, and decide whether or not the project needs to be modified according to the dimensions of the trunk. Cut all the wood to length, smooth the sawn ends with sandpaper, and stack the lengths in readiness. Set out the two workbenches in your chosen working area and generally arrange your tools for the task ahead.

You will need

Tools

✔ Pencil, ruler, tape measure, square, and tracing paper

✔ Two portable workbenches

✔ Crosscut saw

✔ Power drill

✔ Drill bits to match the screw size

✔ Hand cross-head screwdriver

✔ Saber saw and sander

✔ Pair of clamps

Materials

(All rough-sawn pine includes excess length for wastage. All the wood is pressure-treated with preservative.)

For a seat 4 ft. 2 in. in diameter

✔ Pine: 2 rough-sawn 2 x 2s, 10 ft. long (legs)

✔ Pine: 2 rough-sawn 1 x 3s, 10 ft. long (top stretchers)

✔ Pine: 2 rough-sawn 2 x 2s, 10 ft. long (linking stretchers)

✔ Pine: 2 pieces 1-x-4 planed and grooved decking, 10 ft. long (decorative frieze)

✔ Pine: 3 pieces 1-x-4 planed and grooved decking, 10 ft. long (seating boards)

✔ Zinc-plated, countersunk cross-head screws: 200 x 2¼-in.-long no. 8

Overall dimensions and general notes

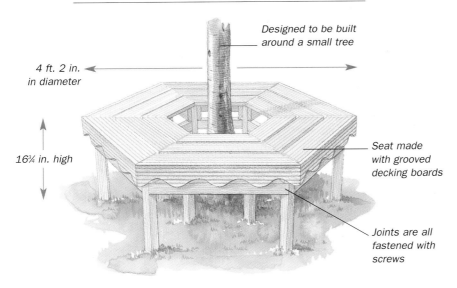

Designed to be built around a small tree

4 ft. 2 in. in diameter

16¾ in. high

Seat made with grooved decking boards

Joints are all fastened with screws

This is a traditional design for freestanding seating to fit around a tree, and it works best on a level site. It could be used to complement the Patio with Sandpit on page 76.

Exploded view of the tree ring seat

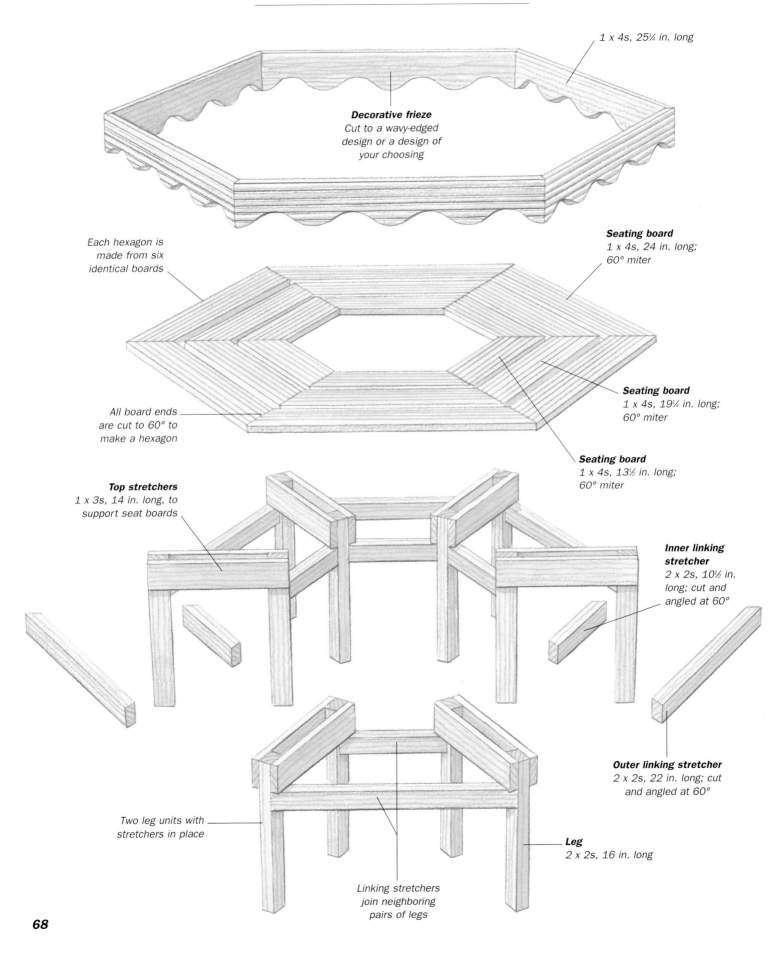

1 x 4s, 25¼ in. long

Decorative frieze
Cut to a wavy-edged design or a design of your choosing

Each hexagon is made from six identical boards

Seating board
1 x 4s, 24 in. long; 60° miter

All board ends are cut to 60° to make a hexagon

Seating board
1 x 4s, 19¼ in. long; 60° miter

Seating board
1 x 4s, 13½ in. long; 60° miter

Top stretchers
1 x 3s, 14 in. long, to support seat boards

Inner linking stretcher
2 x 2s, 10½ in. long; cut and angled at 60°

Outer linking stretcher
2 x 2s, 22 in. long; cut and angled at 60°

Leg
2 x 2s, 16 in. long

Two leg units with stretchers in place

Linking stretchers join neighboring pairs of legs

Making the tree ring seat

1 Making the leg units
Sandwich two legs between two top stretchers, so that you have a frame 16 in. high and 14 in. wide. Fasten each end of each stretcher to the leg with two screws, with the screws offset (see photo). Build six such frames.

2 Fastening the stretchers
When you have made all six leg units, take the inner and outer linking stretchers (all cut to length and angled at 60°) and fasten the units together in pairs, using screws. You should have three identical angle-ended bench units.

3 Joining the structure
Set the three identical bench units around your chosen tree, spacing them to make a hexagon. Fasten the remaining linking stretchers in place with screws to join neighboring bench units.

4 Fitting the seat
Take the seating boards (three different lengths for each of the six sections) and fasten them on top of the frame with screws. Make sure that the sawn ends are centered on the leg frames.

5 Making the decorative frieze
Draw the wavy design on tracing paper and, with a pencil, press-transfer the drawn lines through to the 4-in.-wide frieze boards. Cut out the design with the saber saw and use the sander to smooth the sawn edges.

6 Finishing
Finally, clamp and screw the frieze boards around the seat so that the top edge is flush with the top of the seat. Use the sander on the whole seat area to create a smooth finish.

Adirondack chair

This beautiful folk art chair gets its name from the Adirondack Mountains in upstate New York, where, in the middle of the 19th century, chairs of this type were first made. It is characterized by the flowing shape of the side boards, the roll of the seat, the fan back, and the broad, flat arms. These chairs were originally made from scrap such as crates, salvaged wood, or waste from sawmills.

**Making time
One weekend**
One day for building the basic chair, and one day for finishing

Considering the design

We have modified the basic Adirondack chair design by hinging the arms to the front legs and the seat back, and by fastening a swivel pin between the arms and the fretted side boards so that the chair can be packed flat for winter storage. The design uses only rough-sawn wood, and cutting has been kept to the minimum.

Getting started

Note the various lengths and sections in the working drawings, then saw your wood to size. Stack the wood in four groups: for the basic seat unit, the front legs and arms, the seat back, and the little pieces needed under the seat.

Overall dimensions and general notes

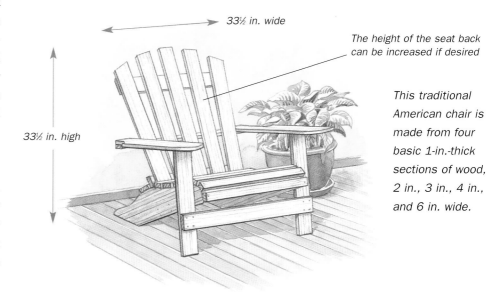

33½ in. wide

33½ in. high

The height of the seat back can be increased if desired

This traditional American chair is made from four basic 1-in.-thick sections of wood, 2 in., 3 in., 4 in., and 6 in. wide.

You will need

Tools

- Pencil, ruler, tape measure, compass, and square
- Two portable workbenches
- Crosscut saw
- Saber saw
- Power drill with a cross-head screwdriver bit
- Drill bits to match the sizes of the screws
- Sander
- Paintbrush

Materials

(All rough-sawn pieces of pine include excess length for wastage. All the wood is pressure-treated with preservative.)

For one chair, 33½ in. wide and 33½ in. high

- Pine: 2 rough-sawn 1 x 6s, 6 ft. 6 in. long (side and arm boards)
- Pine: 3 rough-sawn 1 x 4s, 6 ft. 6 in. long (front legs, stretcher board, stop boards)
- Pine: 6 rough-sawn 1 x 3s, 6 ft. 6 in. long (seat back, back supports, fan support bar, and wide seat boards)
- Pine: 1 rough-sawn 1 x 2, 6 ft. 6 in. long (narrow seat boards)

- Pine: 1 rough-sawn 2 x 2, 3 ft. long, (under-seat fastening blocks)
- Zinc-plated, countersunk cross-head screws: 100 x 1⅝-in.-long no. 8, quantity of ⅝-in.-long no. 8 (number to fit your chosen hinges), 2 x 4-in.-long no. 10 (with washers to fit)
- Hinges: 4 painted 8-in.-long T-hinges (the type used for gates)
- Exterior-grade white masonry paint in a matte finish
- Danish oil

Perspective view of the Adirondack chair

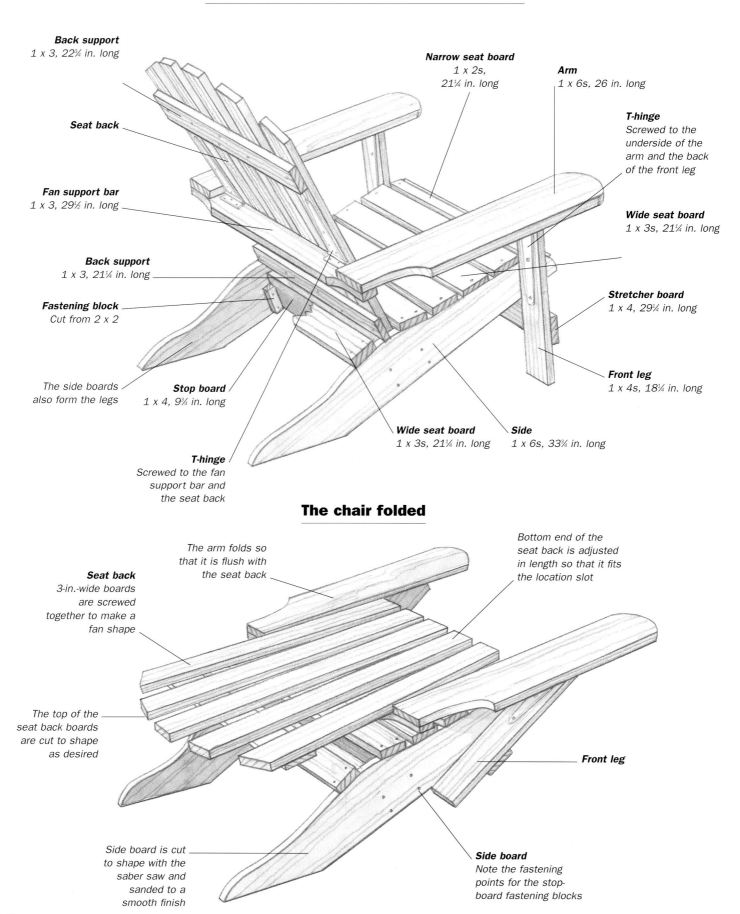

Back support
1 x 3, 22¾ in. long

Seat back

Fan support bar
1 x 3, 29½ in. long

Back support
1 x 3, 21¼ in. long

Fastening block
Cut from 2 x 2

The side boards also form the legs

Stop board
1 x 4, 9¾ in. long

T-hinge
Screwed to the fan support bar and the seat back

Narrow seat board
1 x 2s, 21¼ in. long

Arm
1 x 6s, 26 in. long

T-hinge
Screwed to the underside of the arm and the back of the front leg

Wide seat board
1 x 3s, 21¼ in. long

Stretcher board
1 x 4, 29¼ in. long

Front leg
1 x 4s, 18¼ in. long

Wide seat board
1 x 3s, 21¼ in. long

Side
1 x 6s, 33¾ in. long

The chair folded

The arm folds so that it is flush with the seat back

Seat back
3-in.-wide boards are screwed together to make a fan shape

The top of the seat back boards are cut to shape as desired

Bottom end of the seat back is adjusted in length so that it fits the location slot

Front leg

Side board is cut to shape with the saber saw and sanded to a smooth finish

Side board
Note the fastening points for the stop-board fastening blocks

The chair components

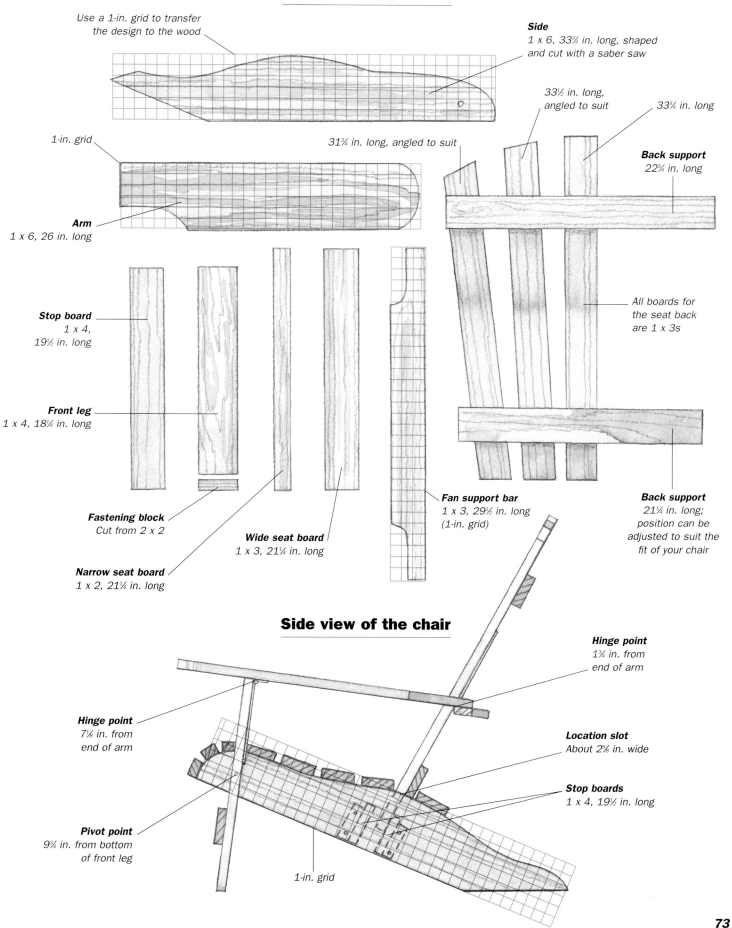

Use a 1-in. grid to transfer the design to the wood

Side
1 x 6, 33¾ in. long, shaped and cut with a saber saw

33½ in. long, angled to suit

33¾ in. long

1-in. grid

31¾ in. long, angled to suit

Back support
22¾ in. long

Arm
1 x 6, 26 in. long

All boards for the seat back are 1 x 3s

Stop board
1 x 4,
19½ in. long

Front leg
1 x 4, 18¼ in. long

Fastening block
Cut from 2 x 2

Wide seat board
1 x 3, 21¼ in. long

Fan support bar
1 x 3, 29½ in. long
(1-in. grid)

Back support
21¼ in. long;
position can be adjusted to suit the fit of your chair

Narrow seat board
1 x 2, 21¼ in. long

Side view of the chair

Hinge point
1¾ in. from end of arm

Hinge point
7⅛ in. from end of arm

Location slot
About 2⅝ in. wide

Stop boards
1 x 4, 19½ in. long

Pivot point
9¾ in. from bottom of front leg

1-in. grid

73

Making the Adirondack chair

1 Cutting the boards

Draw curves on the appropriate boards for the two arms, the two side boards, the five seat back boards, and the single fan support bar that links the ends of the arms across the chair back. Use the saber saw to cut out the shapes.

2 Making the seat

To form the seat, take three narrow seat boards and four wide seat boards, and fasten them to the two side boards with 1³⁄₈-in.-long screws. (A final wide seat board is added later.) The two sides must be parallel to each other and square with the seat.

3 Making the legs

Take the two boards that make the front legs, link them with the stretcher board—to make the characteristic H-frame—and fasten them with four 1³⁄₈-in.-long screws at each intersection.

4 Hinging the arms

Set the two arms face down, and hinge them to the front H-frame. Note that the stretcher board is placed so that it lies across the front of the legs.

5 Attaching the fan support

Screw the fan support bar to the back ends of the two arm boards, all the while making sure that all the components are square to each other.

6 Pivoting the seat

Drill pivot holes through the side boards. Slide the washers on the 4-in.-long screws and drive the screws through the side board holes and into the thickness of the front legs.

7 Making the location slot

Position the chair so that the top of the seat is uppermost, and screw the eighth seat board in place with $1^3/_8$-in.-long screws. Leave a $2^5/_8$-in. gap between the eighth board and the one before it to make the location slot for the seat back.

8 Fastening the stop boards

With the underside of the seat uppermost, fasten the two stop boards (to secure the seat back in the location slot) in place with $1^3/_8$-in.-long screws and the under-seat fastening blocks. Screw the blocks to the stop boards first, then screw the blocks to the side boards.

9 Making the back

Take the five seat back boards, and place them good face down, arranging them into a fan shape. The spread of the fan at the bottom edge of back support bar must not exceed $19^1/_2$ in.. Screw the two back supports in place with $1^3/_8$-in.-long screws.

10 Fastening the back

Slide the seat back into the location slot, raise the arms so that it is supported, and hinge the seat back to the fan support bar with $5/_8$-in.-long screws. Paint the chair, let it dry, sand it down so that it edges look worn, then give it a coat of Danish oil.

Patio with sandpit

Picture this: the sun is shining, you are relaxed and stretched out on wooden decking, there is a dappled canopy of leaves overhead, and there is a child at your side happily playing in a sandpit. If you choose this project, that scene could become reality after a weekend's work. The structure measures 9 feet 6 inches long by 6 feet 6 inches wide, but there is no reason why you cannot make it bigger or smaller to suit your garden.

Making time
One weekend
One day for the basic structure, and one day for fastening the decking and finishing

Considering the design

There are holes to accommodate the sandpit and a tree. The decking boards are slightly cut back around the sandpit, so that the resultant board-thickness step between the surface of the decking and the top face of the beam becomes the lip for the pet-proof hatch cover. Because children will be crawling over the decking, make sure that a sealant is used over the preserved wood.

Getting started

Inspect your site and choose a level area with a suitable tree. Measure the girth of the tree, and decide just where the sandpit will be placed. Choose your wood with extra care, and make sure that it is free from loose knots and splits.

Overall dimensions and general notes

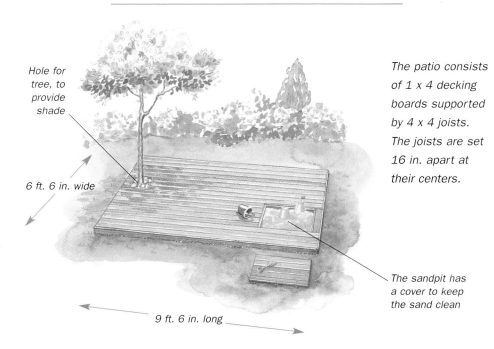

Hole for tree, to provide shade

6 ft. 6 in. wide

9 ft. 6 in. long

The patio consists of 1 x 4 decking boards supported by 4 x 4 joists. The joists are set 16 in. apart at their centers.

The sandpit has a cover to keep the sand clean

You will need

Tools

- ✔ Pencil, ruler, tape measure, square
- ✔ Pegs and string
- ✔ Two portable workbenches
- ✔ Crosscut saw
- ✔ Power drill with a cross-head screwdriver bit
- ✔ Drill bit to match the size of screws
- ✔ Claw hammer
- ✔ Sander
- ✔ Paintbrush

Materials

(All rough-sawn pieces of pine include excess length for wastage. All the wood is pressure-treated with preservative)

For a patio 9 ft. 6 in. long and 6 ft. 6 in. wide

- ✔ Pine: 8 rough-sawn 4 x 4s, 6 ft. 6 in. long (joists)
- ✔ Pine: 22 rough-sawn 1 x 4s, 10 ft. long (decking boards, frames, fascias)
- ✔ Pine: 1 rough-sawn 1 x 2, 6 ft. 6 in. long (sandpit hatch cover strips)

- ✔ Plastic ground sheet: 10 ft. long and 6 ft. 6 in. wide (to go under decking)
- ✔ Nails: 2 lb. of 5-in.-long (40 d) nails
- ✔ Zinc-plated, countersunk cross-head screws: 300 x 2-in.-long no. 8, 50 x 1⅜-in.-long no.8
- ✔ Matte decking sealant
- ✔ Well-graded mortar sand: 110 lb. clean, washed sand

Exploded view of the patio with sandpit

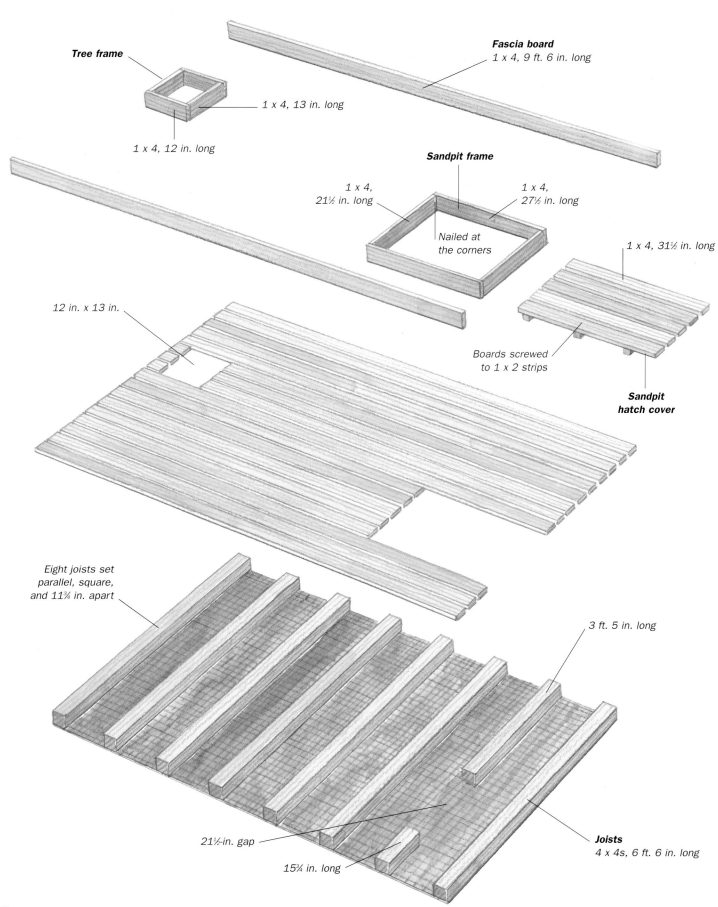

Tree frame

1 x 4, 13 in. long

1 x 4, 12 in. long

Fascia board
1 x 4, 9 ft. 6 in. long

Sandpit frame

1 x 4,
21½ in. long

1 x 4,
27½ in. long

*Nailed at
the corners*

1 x 4, 31½ in. long

12 in. x 13 in.

Boards screwed
to 1 x 2 strips

**Sandpit
hatch cover**

Eight joists set
parallel, square,
and 11¾ in. apart

3 ft. 5 in. long

21½-in. gap

15¾ in. long

Joists
4 x 4s, 6 ft. 6 in. long

Exploded view of the patio with sandpit

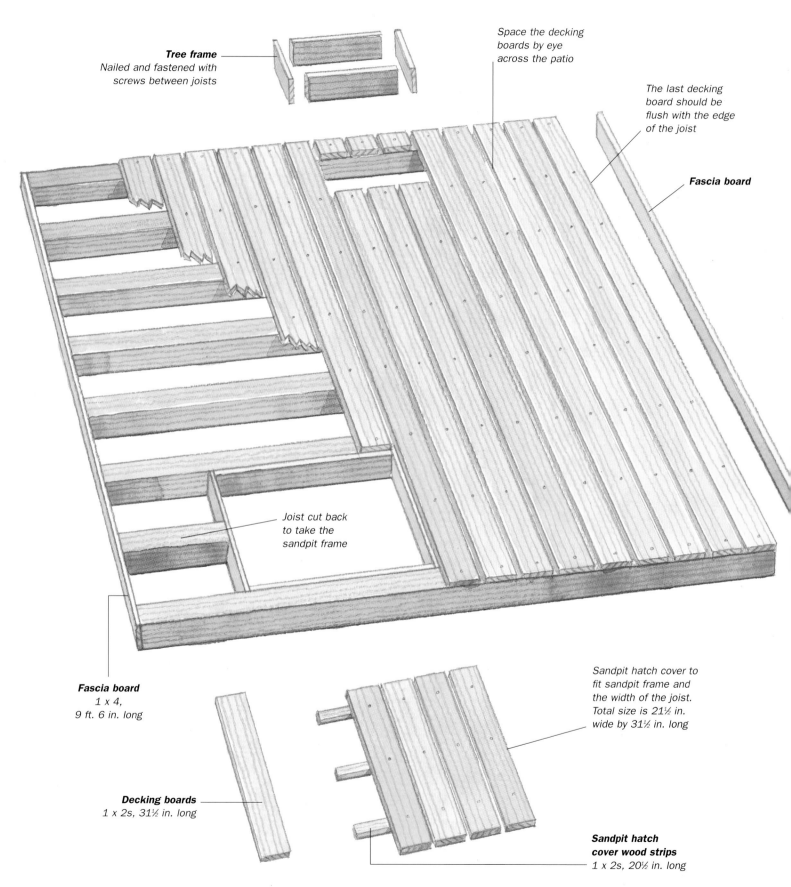

Tree frame
Nailed and fastened with
screws between joists

Space the decking
boards by eye
across the patio

The last decking
board should be
flush with the edge
of the joist

Fascia board

Joist cut back
to take the
sandpit frame

Fascia board
1 x 4,
9 ft. 6 in. long

Decking boards
1 x 2s, 31½ in. long

Sandpit hatch cover to
fit sandpit frame and
the width of the joist.
Total size is 21½ in.
wide by 31½ in. long

**Sandpit hatch
cover wood strips**
1 x 2s, 20½ in. long

Making the patio with sandpit

1 Cutting the joists
Cut the joists to length (allowing for the sandpit area), and set them in position on the site, together with a couple of decking boards, to give you an idea of how the finished project will look. Decide exactly where they will lie in relation to the tree.

2 Fastening the joists
Cover the whole site with the plastic ground sheet, leaving a hole around the tree. Position the joists, setting them square with the plastic and parallel to each other. Fasten them in place with a decking board at each side, using one screw at each intersection.

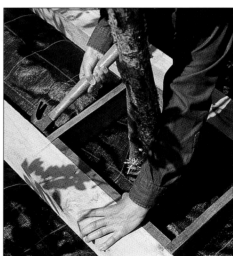

3 Squaring the frame
To ensure that the frame is square, measure the diagonals and make adjustments to the frame until both diagonals are equal. Drive in a second screw at each corner.

4 Making the frames
Build two frames—a tree frame to go around the tree, and a sandpit frame for the sandpit. Nail and screw the frames in place between the joists.

5 Fastening the decking
Cut and fit all the long decking boards, which run the full length of the frame. Fasten them to the joists with screws. Set them flush with the sides of the two frames. Leave a 21½-in. gap between the boards for the sandpit, and a 13-in. gap for the tree.

6 Completing the decking
Cut and fit all the other shorter decking boards, spacing them as before. They should be stepped back around the sandpit frame to provide a lip for the sandpit hatch cover, and flush with the tree frame. Cut boards for the sandpit hatch cover.

7 Fastening the fascia boards
Fit the fascia boards along the two long sides of the decking, covering the ends of the joists. Position the edges of the boards so that they are flush with the surface of the decking.

8 Making the sandpit hatch cover
Fasten the boards for the sandpit hatch cover to the three wood strips. Space them to match the rest of the decking. Finally, sand down the structure with the sander, give all the surfaces two or three coats of a matte sealant, and fill the sandpit.

Hillside decking

This decking is designed specifically to be built on a piece of gently sloping ground. You simply cut the posts to length to suit the slope, then bolt them to the platform and set them in concrete. Working in this way, it is easy to adapt the structure to suit just about any situation. The project is made up from three basic platforms: one set at ground level, one set higher up the slope, and a mini platform that is used as a step.

Making time
One long weekend
One day for the frames, and one day for fitting and fastening the posts, and finishing

Considering the design

The joists are butted and screwed at the corners, then bolted to the posts. The upper platform is set at a 45-degree angle to the lower one. The three platforms are built as separate units, which allows you to change them around to suit the slope and layout of your garden.

Getting started

Decide how you want the platforms to be positioned in relation to each other. If you find it difficult to picture, build the lower one and set it in the ground, then build the upper one and move it around until you find a suitable position.

Overall dimensions and general notes

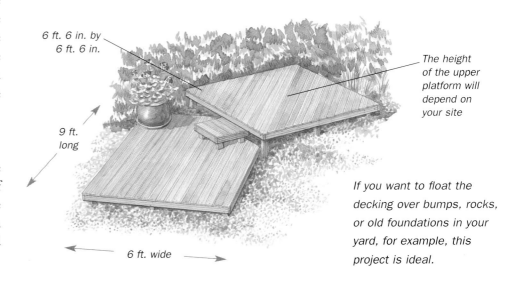

6 ft. 6 in. by 6 ft. 6 in.

9 ft. long

6 ft. wide

The height of the upper platform will depend on your site

If you want to float the decking over bumps, rocks, or old foundations in your yard, for example, this project is ideal.

You will need

Tools

- Pencil, ruler, tape measure, and square
- Two portable workbenches
- Crosscut saw
- Power drill with a cross-head screwdriver bit
- Drill bits to match the sizes of the screws and bolts
- Spade
- Wrench to fit the bolts
- Wheelbarrow
- Bucket
- Shovel and pointing trowel

- Spirit level
- Sledgehammer
- Sander

Materials

(All rough-sawn pieces of pine include excess length for wastage. All the wood is pressure-treated with preservative.)

For two areas of decking: 6 ft. by 9 ft., and 6 ft. 6 in. square

- Pine: 5 rough-sawn 3 x 3s, 6 ft. 6 in. long (posts)
- Pine: 22 rough-sawn 2 x 4s, 6 ft. 6 in. long; two 2 x 4s, 10 ft. long (joists, frames, and blockings)

- Pine: 34 rough-sawn 2 x 4s, 10 ft. long (decking boards)
- Pine: 2 rough-sawn 1 x 2s, 10 ft. long (temporary bracing strips)
- Zinc-plated, countersunk cross-head screws: 300 x 1⅝-in.-long no. 8, 100 x 3½-in.-long. no. 10
- Zinc-plated carriage bolts with nuts and washers to fit 30 x 6-in.-long bolts
- Concrete: 1 part (110 lb.) Portland cement, 2 parts (220 lb.) sand, 3 parts (330 lb.) aggregate

Exploded view of the hillside decking

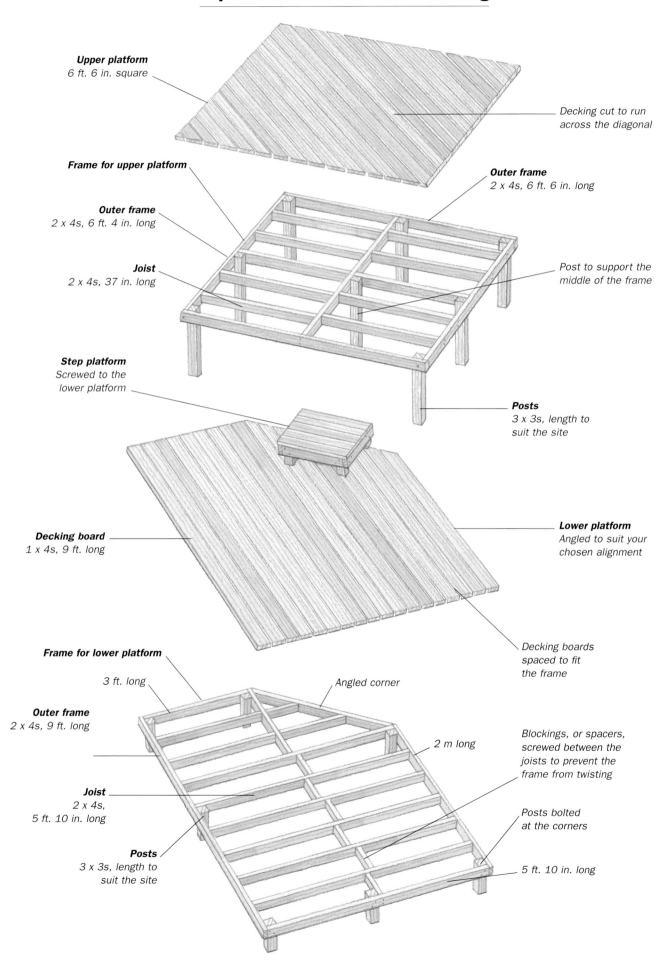

Upper platform
6 ft. 6 in. square

Decking cut to run
across the diagonal

Frame for upper platform

Outer frame
2 x 4s, 6 ft. 6 in. long

Outer frame
2 x 4s, 6 ft. 4 in. long

Joist
2 x 4s, 37 in. long

Post to support the
middle of the frame

Step platform
Screwed to the
lower platform

Posts
3 x 3s, length to
suit the site

Decking board
1 x 4s, 9 ft. long

Lower platform
Angled to suit your
chosen alignment

Decking boards
spaced to fit
the frame

Frame for lower platform

3 ft. long

Angled corner

Outer frame
2 x 4s, 9 ft. long

2 m long

Blockings, or spacers,
screwed between the
joists to prevent the
frame from twisting

Joist
2 x 4s,
5 ft. 10 in. long

Posts bolted
at the corners

Posts
3 x 3s, length to
suit the site

5 ft. 10 in. long

Plan view of the hillside decking

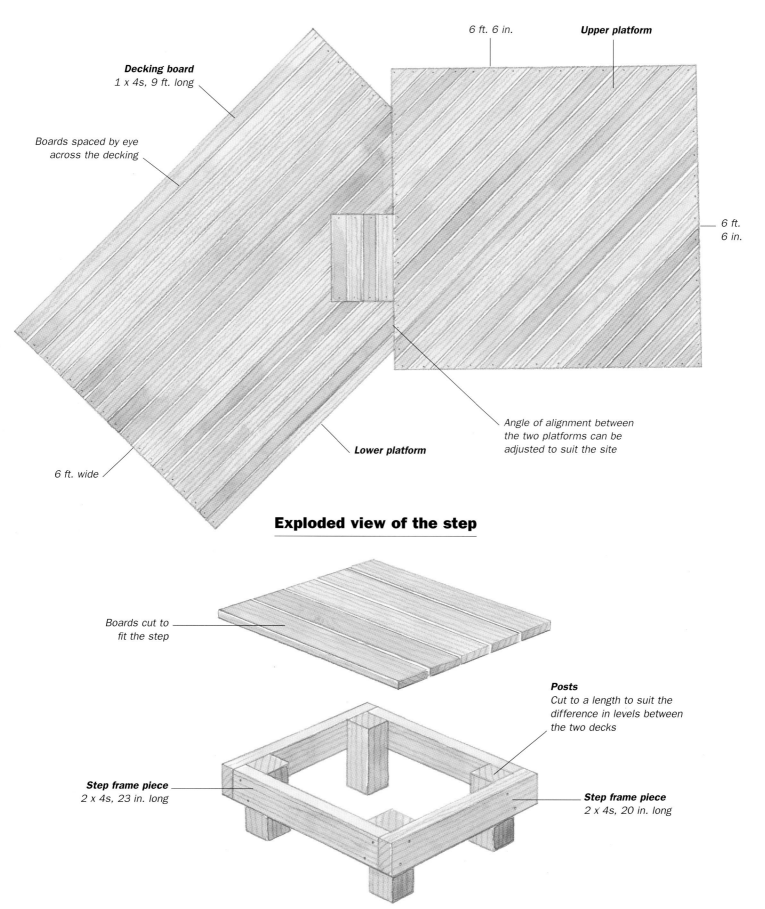

Decking board
1 x 4s, 9 ft. long

Boards spaced by eye
across the decking

6 ft. wide

6 ft. 6 in.

Upper platform

6 ft.
6 in.

Lower platform

Angle of alignment between
the two platforms can be
adjusted to suit the site

Exploded view of the step

Boards cut to
fit the step

Posts
Cut to a length to suit the
difference in levels between
the two decks

Step frame piece
2 x 4s, 23 in. long

Step frame piece
2 x 4s, 20 in. long

Making the hillside decking

1 Planning
Use the joists to plan out the total design on the ground. Work out the precise dimensions of the lower platform and the position of the post holes.

2 Lower platform frame
Cut the wood for the outer frame, butt the pieces at the corners, and fasten with 3½-in.-long screws. Cut the diagonal piece for the angled corner to suit the frame. Fit in place. With 1⅝-in.-long screws, fasten temporary bracings across the diagonals to hold the frame square.

3 Fitting the joists
Cut the joists and place them inside the outer frame so that they are set a little over 12 in. apart at their centers. Fasten each joint with two 3½-in.-long screws.

5 Attaching the posts
Bolt the posts to the frame, so that the tops are just level with the top of the frame. Repeat all the procedures just described to make the upper platform, then set it in place.

4 Digging the post holes
Set the frame level on the ground and establish the position of the posts within the frame. Dig a 12-in.-deep hole for each post. Set the posts in place and trim them to length to suit the height of the frame off the ground.

6 Checking levels

Check each frame with the spirit level to make sure that it is horizontal, and make any small adjustments either by using the sledgehammer to tap down the posts, or by wedging the frames with shims or thin pieces of scrap wood.

7 Concreting the posts

Set both frames in their post holes. Mix a stiff batch of concrete, and tamp it into the holes around the posts, filling them almost to ground level. Trowel the concrete flush with the ground and shape it so that rainwater will flow away from the posts.

8 Fastening the decking

Screw the decking boards across the upper platform frame with 1⅝-in.-long screws, so that they are at 45° to the sides. Use the crosscut saw to trim the waste ends so that they run parallel to the frame. Fit decking boards to the lower platform.

9 Building the step

Repeat the procedures in Steps 1–8 to build a small platform to act as a step (modify to suit your decking). Screw the step to the lower platform with 3½-in.-long screws, driving the screws down through the legs at an angle. Finally, sand everything to a smooth finish.

Waterside raised decking

Raised decking is a wonderfully exciting feature for a yard that backs onto a stretch of water. It's a magical feeling to be raised up high and looking out over a lake, river, or the sea. This project is time-consuming and a challenge, but the design is easy to understand. The order of work is to first set the posts in concrete, bolt a frame to the posts to establish the level of the decking, then fill in the frame with joists.

Making time
Two weekends
One weekend for the basic frame; second weekend for the balusters and details

Considering the design

Decking is laid over the joists, the posts are trimmed to establish the level of the handrail, then the balusters are made.

Getting started

Only 6 of the 10 posts are set in the ground, but in your particular situation this may vary: study your site, decide where the decking is going, and see how many posts need to be set in concrete.

Overall dimensions and general notes

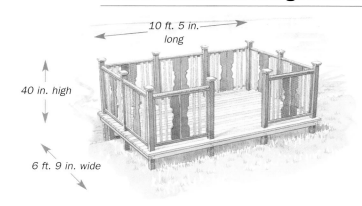

10 ft. 5 in. long

40 in. high

6 ft. 9 in. wide

This decking is designed to be built on a riverbank, or it could overhang a pond. You can choose where the baluster rail panels go—the entrance can be moved.

You will need

Tools

Warning: Because you are working by water, power tools must be used with a ground-fault circuit interrupter (GFCI).

- ✔ Pencil, ruler, tape measure, square
- ✔ Two portable workbenches
- ✔ Crosscut saw
- ✔ Spade and shovel
- ✔ Wrench to fit your chosen nuts
- ✔ Sledgehammer
- ✔ Spirit level
- ✔ Power drill with a cross-head screwdriver bit
- ✔ Drill bits to match the sizes of the screws and bolts
- ✔ Wheelbarrow, bucket, and trowel
- ✔ Saber saw
- ✔ Pair of clamps
- ✔ Sander

Materials

(All rough-sawn pieces of pine include excess length for wastage and design modifications. All the wood is pressure-treated with preservative.)

For raised decking 10 ft. 5 in. long, 6 ft. 9 in. wide, and 40 in. high

- ✔ Pine: 14 rough-sawn 3 x 3s, 10 ft. long (10 main posts and secondary posts, joist supports, bracing beams)
- ✔ Pine: 15 rough-sawn 2 x 4s, 10 ft. long (joists, blockings, temporary bracing strips)
- ✔ Pine: 27 1-x-5 planed-and-grooved decking board, 10 ft. long (floor and any steps that might be needed)
- ✔ Pine: 15 rough-sawn 1 x 2s, 10 ft. long (baluster rails and fastening strips)
- ✔ Pine: 4 rough-sawn 1 x 3s, 10 ft. long (pitch-topped rail capping)

- ✔ Pine: 15 rough-sawn 1 x 2s, 6 ft. 6 in. long (slender balusters or vertical rails)
- ✔ Pine: 12 rough-sawn 1 x 6s, 10 ft. long (wide, fretted baluster boards and newel post caps)
- ✔ Zinc-plated carriage bolts with washers and nuts to fit: 36 x 4¾-in.-long bolts, 16 x 7-in.-long bolts
- ✔ Zinc-plated, countersunk cross-head screws: 400 x 3½-in.-long no. 8, 400 x 3-in.-long no. 10
- ✔ Concrete: 1 part (110 lb.) Portland cement, 2 parts (220 lb.) sand, 3 parts (330 lb.) aggregate
- ✔ Gravel: 1 bucket for each post

Exploded view of the waterside raised decking

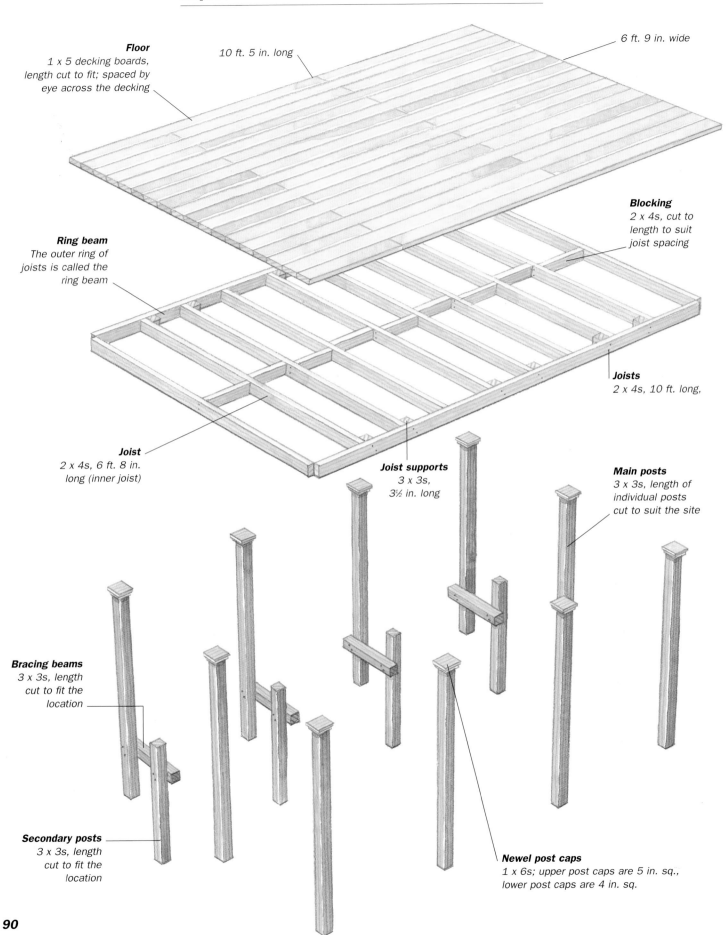

Floor
1 x 5 decking boards, length cut to fit; spaced by eye across the decking

10 ft. 5 in. long

6 ft. 9 in. wide

Blocking
2 x 4s, cut to length to suit joist spacing

Ring beam
The outer ring of joists is called the ring beam

Joists
2 x 4s, 10 ft. long,

Joist
2 x 4s, 6 ft. 8 in. long (inner joist)

Joist supports
3 x 3s, 3½ in. long

Main posts
3 x 3s, length of individual posts cut to suit the site

Bracing beams
3 x 3s, length cut to fit the location

Secondary posts
3 x 3s, length cut to fit the location

Newel post caps
1 x 6s; upper post caps are 5 in. sq., lower post caps are 4 in. sq.

Front view of the waterside raised decking (viewed from the water)

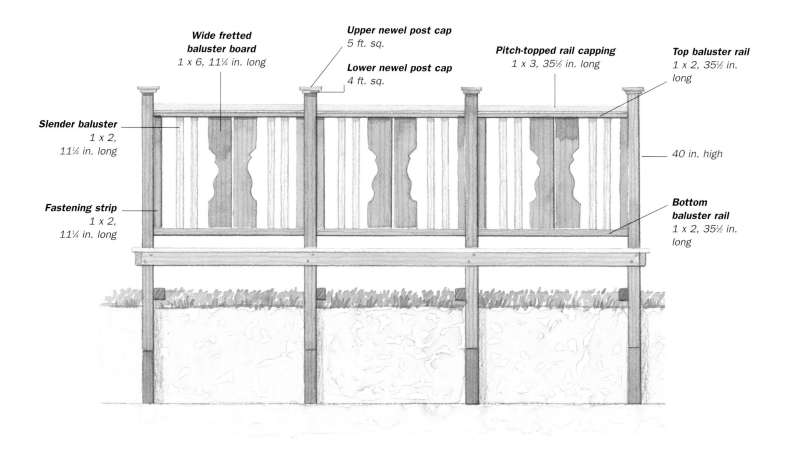

Wide fretted baluster board
1 x 6, 11¼ in. long

Upper newel post cap
5 ft. sq.

Lower newel post cap
4 ft. sq.

Pitch-topped rail capping
1 x 3, 35½ in. long

Top baluster rail
1 x 2, 35½ in. long

Slender baluster
1 x 2, 11¼ in. long

Fastening strip
1 x 2, 11¼ in. long

40 in. high

Bottom baluster rail
1 x 2, 35½ in. long

Side view of the waterside raised decking

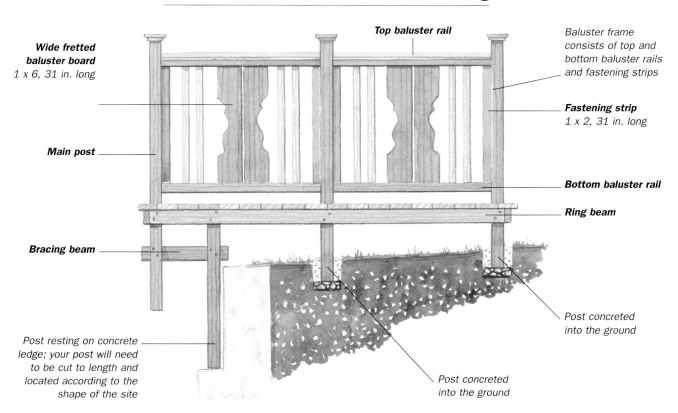

Wide fretted baluster board
1 x 6, 31 in. long

Top baluster rail

Baluster frame consists of top and bottom baluster rails and fastening strips

Fastening strip
1 x 2, 31 in. long

Main post

Bottom baluster rail

Ring beam

Bracing beam

Post concreted into the ground

Post resting on concrete ledge; your post will need to be cut to length and located according to the shape of the site

Post concreted into the ground

Making the waterside raised decking

1 Digging post holes

Dig holes for the main posts that require them, to a depth of 12 in. Set the main posts in them. Loosely bolt the outer ring of joists (ring beam) to the main posts and outer secondary posts to create the frame.

2 Leveling

With the spirit level, check that the ring beam is level. Adjust the height of individual posts if necessary, by standing them on gravel. (Compact the gravel with the sledgehammer.) Use the wrench to tightly clench the bolts holding the posts to the ring beam.

3 Concreting the posts

Fasten the inner joists in place in the frame with 3$\frac{1}{2}$-in.-long screws, along with blockings and joist supports. Check that the whole structure is square. Make a stiff mixture of concrete and pour it into the post holes around the posts. Trowel to a smooth finish.

4 Fitting the secondary posts

Using carriage bolts, fasten the secondary posts, bracing beams, and braces. Saw off the secondary posts level with the joists. Saw off the main posts level with each other, and screw a temporary bracing across the top to hold them square.

6 Cutting the wide balusters

Draw the decorative profile on the 6-in.-wide boards and use the saber saw to cut out the shape. Sand the sawn edges to a smooth finish.

5 Fastening the floor

Fasten the decking boards across the frame of joists with 3-in.-long screws, making sure that the joints between boards are staggered. Cut and fasten the boards at the edge so that you see a nosing as you approach the decking from the yard.

7 Making the baluster frames

Make up the baluster frames on the ground, complete with fastening strips, top and bottom baluster rails, pitch-topped rail capping, slender balusters, and wide fretted balusters. Fasten together with 3-in.-long screws.

8 Finishing

Clamp the baluster frames between the posts and fasten them with 3½-in.-long screws. Cut and fasten the upper and lower newel post caps to the top of the posts with 3-in.-long screws. Finally, smooth down the whole structure with the sander.

Glossary

Aligning
Setting one component part against another and obtaining a good fit or alignment of the two.

Back-filling
Filling post holes with gravel and/or concrete in order to stabilize the posts. Also to fill the area surrounding the post to raise it to the desired level.

Bracing
Minimizing any sideways or skewing movement in a structure by adding a secondary member to triangulate it.

Butting
Pushing one component part snugly against another in order to obtain a good, flush fit, with both faces touching.

Centering
Marking and placing a component in the center of another. Also, measuring from the center of one component to the center of another.

Cladding
Covering a frame with decking boards.

Dry run
Putting part of a project together without nails, screws, or bolts in order to see whether or not the components will fit and to make sure that the design will work successfully.

Finishing
The final procedure, at the end of a project, of sanding, painting, staining, oiling, or washing down in order to complete the project.

Framing
Fastening horizontal joists and beams to vertical posts.

Jointing
The procedure of fastening one length of wood to another by means of screws, nails, bolts, or a traditional cut woodworking joint.

Leveling
Using a spirit level to decide whether or not a component part is horizontally parallel to the ground or vertically at right angles to the ground, then making adjustments to bring the component into line.

Marking out
Variously using a pencil, rule, square, compass, and pegs and string to draw lines on a piece of wood or mark out an area on the ground in readiness for cutting or otherwise working on a project.

Planning and designing
The whole procedure of considering a project—from looking at the materials to making drawings and working out amounts and costs—prior to actually starting work.

Sawing to size
Taking sawn wood (meaning wood that has been purchased ready sawn to width and thickness) and cutting it to length.

Sighting
To judge by eye, or to look down a tool or a length of wood, to determine whether or not a cut, joint, or structure is level or true.

Siting
The act of walking around the yard and taking everything into consideration in order to decide where a project should be placed.

Sourcing
The process of questioning suppliers by phone, visit, letter, or e-mail in order to ascertain the best source for materials.

Squaring
The technique of marking out, with a set square and/or spirit level, to make sure that one surface or structure is at right angles to another.

Squaring a frame
Ensuring squareness (90-degree corners) in a rectangular frame by measuring across the diagonals and making adjustments until both diagonals are identical—at which point the frame is square.

Trimming
The act of bringing wood to a smooth finish with sandpaper and paint. Also, a technique for preventing a frame from becoming skewed, by adding blockings or trimming pieces.

Index

AG&G Books would like to
thank Garden and Wildlife
Matters Photographic Library
for contributing the photographs
used on pages 6, 7, and 18-23.